COURAGE

COURAGE: MY JOURNEY THROUGH GRIEF AFTER THE DEATH OF OUR CHILD © Karen Lang

National Library of Australia Cataloguing-in-Publication entry (pbk)

Creator:	Lang, Karen, author.
Title:	Courage: My journey through grief after the death of our child / Karen Lang.
ISBN:	978-0-6486386-0-5 (paperback)
Subjects:	Lang, Nathan.
	Sons–Death–Biography.
	Child traffic fatalities–Australia–Biography
	Parental grief–Biography.
	Spiritual healing.
	Mind and body.

COURAGE

MY JOURNEY THROUGH GRIEF
AFTER THE DEATH OF OUR CHILD

KAREN LANG

The root of the word courage is cor—
the Latin word for heart.
Our courage is deep within our heart.

The dragonfly symbolizes the meaning of metamorphosis and transformation, it inspires us to initiate the changes needed in our lives, in order to reach our full potential.

For my son, Nathan, who had a heart filled with courage and love.

His death taught me how precious life is and how to live more fully.

TABLE OF CONTENTS

PART THREE   125

PART FOUR   157

Karen Lang's book *Courage* beautifully illustrates the truth in the saying, "There is life after death". Karen's honest, uncomplicated, and insightful words have captured the living proof of this statement.

While the death of a child is one of the most harrowing and life altering experiences any mother can experience, Karen has found a way to appeal to readers embarking on this journey themselves, and to draw them alongside each footstep of her personal journey towards hope. Through her journey, Karen makes it seem just a little more possible that we can take the next breath; that we can wake up the next morning; that we can live through this agonizing and cruel life process; and maybe, in our own time and own way, we can even flourish.

Grief is as unique to individuals as their fingerprints. *Courage* is Karen's story; it is her truth and a thoughtful collection of her life lessons.

Courage is a book that breathes life back into a suffocating experience and I would recommend it, and will use it in my own work with families experiencing the death of a child.

Gabrielle Quilliam
Co-founder Hummingbird House
(Queensland's only children's hospice)

Following the death of her son Nathan in a tragic accident, Karen Lang's life was instantly one of loss, turmoil, and deep grief. But through courage, determination, and spirituality over the following dark years, Karen managed to find a renewed purpose and meaning in her life, but always with Nathan in her heart and memory. *Courage* is an inspirational story of a mother's journey from utter despair and hopelessness to strength and rebirth.

Tilly Brasch - Author
No Middle Name - Glass House Books

Thank you for the trust that you have placed in me in allowing me to read your story—Nathan's story. I was deeply moved by your writing. What has impressed me the most is the way that you have structured the book and the sense of resilience and hope that emerges, despite the harrowing loss and trauma.

The way in which you incorporated meditations and mindfulness practices seamlessly into the book makes them more accessible to those reading your book in the wake of their own loss. Your voice is strong and assured in your writing, and you have found a balance between your personal story and universal themes.

Susan Wilson
MBBS UQ (Hons)
FRANZCP, Child and Adolescent Psychiatrist

PREFACE

While death is a natural part of our journey, when we lose a child, our lives change forever. In the shock and grief of my loss, I questioned everything I had ever believed. Nothing in life had prepared me. I had no coping skills for this journey and nothing seemed real.

At first, I did not understand how I could survive, and there was no way out of the endlessness of the pain. Yet, over time, I found a way.

As I worked through the raw emotions of grief, I allowed myself to experience the pain and confront my reality. I observed changes in my relationships, in how I saw myself, and in how I perceived my purpose in the world; and ultimately, I gave myself time to understand and nurture these feelings.

Throughout this book, I have provided ways to identify and understand the intricate layers of grief. It is my hope that this story will help others find the courage to heal. May you find comfort in knowing that you are not alone.

INTRODUCTION

After our son's funeral, we were overwhelmed with condolences, cards, and flowers. As I began reading each card, there was one that touched me deeply. It was from a lady I had met a few years earlier. She explained that she too had lost a child—a three year-old daughter who had died from a brain tumor. She wrote, 'Although this is a very difficult journey, I promise you will survive this'. I remember feeling the power behind her words and sat there for a long time contemplating them. Her belief in me gave me hope and perhaps the confidence to step out into the wild terrain of grief.

As I embarked on this journey, I learned there was no single way to heal, but discovered multiple platforms of support and understanding. My book offers a holistic approach to grief and I share my experiences with complimentary therapies such as yoga and meditation, but also include counseling as integral parts of my support.

I was never the same after Nathan died. Although I hoped my life would return to normal, it wasn't until I accepted a new world without my son that I was able to start healing. Part of accepting this new life was discovered alongside my passion as a counselor.

I realized that because I was experiencing this journey, I understood it, and in turn, I developed a desire to help others who were searching for answers as I was. My own independent study, in the wake of my grief, led me to study a Diploma in Counseling formally. With a background in nursing, it seemed natural to want to help those in need, but I knew I could never guide anyone towards healing until I had worked through my own grief first.

Healing grief after losing a child spans a life time; and although this seems daunting at first, I found that I only needed to live one day at a time. Over the years, I began to see beyond my pain and into a hopeful future.

I hope you discover many ways to heal in this book. Each story of loss is unique. Be patient finding the right people to support you, but most of all, do it in your own way and in your own time.

PART ONE

THE ACCIDENT

❝Your pain is the breaking
of the shell that encloses
your understanding.❞
Kahlil Gibran

On Thursday morning, Nathan woke up and asked for the day off school. Nathan loved school and never asked to stay home. That morning, however, he followed me around the house insisting that he needed a break. I had several meetings scheduled and had committed to help organize a fundraising event for his school, so I went to speak to my husband, Michael. He was in the bathroom getting ready for work. I said, "Natty really wants a day off. What do you think?"

We went back and forth about it but since he wasn't sick, we said no. Nathan was disappointed but he got ready and off we went.

The day went ahead as planned and that afternoon, I picked up the kids from school and got ready for their sporting commitments. That night, after putting Nathan to bed, he called out. I had already kissed him goodnight and so I answered, "What is it?"

He said he was scared and that he wanted me to lie with him. I will always remember that I said, "Nathan, you are fine. I'm tired. Go to sleep."

After work the next day, I went to pick up Nathan and my five year-old daughter, Lauren. All day I had a headache. The pain was so intense that it made me feel uneasy, like something was wrong. In hindsight, there were many signs—signs from Nathan and the universe—to stop, but I didn't. It was Friday afternoon and we all looked forward to a relaxing weekend.

As I walked up to school, Nathan rushed to tell me that he had received full marks on his spelling test. He was excited because I had promised him that if he did well, I would buy him some *Dragonball Z* cards. He loved sharing the cards with his friends.

We left school and headed to our good friend Katrina's home, picking up Nathan's new cards on the way. When we arrived at Katrina's, we parked across from her house. I told Nathan and Lauren to wait for me. I opened the back door to get our bags and drinks. In his excitement to see his friends, Nathan jumped out of the front seat and ran across the road, oblivious to the oncoming car.

As I looked up, our eyes locked. The sound of the car hitting his body would stay with me forever.

I dropped everything and ran to his side. I knew it was bad. He was unconscious and there was blood coming out of his nose and ear. He let out a moan. I comforted him, stroked his face, and let him know that I was there. I told him everything would be okay.

My friends came running out to the street. One rang an ambulance and Michael. Another took Lauren into the house. The lady across the road came running out with a blanket and I placed it over him. He felt cold.

The ambulance arrived quickly but I am not sure I noticed. I kept saying, "I am here, Nathan. It will be okay."

The paramedics called another ambulance when they saw his condition. I asked the paramedic checking Nathan, "Is it bad?" and as he looked at me, I saw his fear.

He replied simply, "It's bad."

As the paramedics assessed his injuries and tried to put an IV into his arm, his heart stopped. Nathan was lying on the side of the road when the driver of the car who hit him appeared. She told the paramedics she was a nurse. I was aware she was next to me, but in my shock from the accident, my only focus was on Nathan. She began performing CPR with them. I felt helpless as I gently rubbed his foot.

The paramedics got his heart going again and rushed him to the hospital. I travelled ahead in the first ambulance and they took Nathan in the second. My mind raced as the sirens echoed through the streets. A medical team stood outside the emergency entrance, immediately attending to Nathan's injuries. A CAT scan was booked and I was told that the neurologist was on his way.

Michael and my sister, Sheryl, arrived through the emergency room doors, desperate to see Nathan, and find out what happened. While the neurologist assessed my son, I asked, "Is it bad that his pupils are dilated?"

"It depends," was all he said. I stopped asking questions after that.

Michael and I stood silently together, enveloped in shock and disbelief. We felt completely helpless and desperate as the medical team attended to Nathan and as I looked over at his precious face, I realized how quickly nine years had passed.

NATHAN

"*Every child begins the world again.*"
Henry David Thoreau

Nathan came into the world on a windy day in August 1992 as an emergency. After going a week over my due date, my obstetrician induced me. Many hours passed before there were any signs of labor and when it finally occurred, Nathan's heart rate started to drop. When his heart rate dropped again, the obstetrician decided on an emergency caesarean.

When they opened me up, they found that the umbilical cord was wrapped around Nathan's neck. After recovering from the trauma of Nathan's birth, my husband, Michael, and I were both exhausted and grateful for the safe arrival of our first child.

Nathan was a beautiful, placid baby. He fed well and soon earned the nickname Buddha because of all the chubby rolls he accumulated. Every time we went for a check-up, Nathan was always in the top three percent in weight and height. The doctor said he was surprised that I was only breastfeeding him.

As first time parents, we hovered over Nathan's every move, hoping we were doing our best. I enrolled him in every baby class, believing it was necessary, although I am sure he would have preferred for me to relax a little.

Nathan grew into a mischievous toddler and lost his cute Buddha rolls from all the running around. From the moment the sun rose, Nathan was up playing and made the most of each and every day.

While renovating the house, Nathan's favorite activity was putting on his plastic tool-belt and pretending he was helping Michael. He thought he was so strong and would come up the stairs puffing and telling me he had worked very hard and now needed a rest.

Life was busy with a toddler. Balancing work and renovating kept us on the move, but we got by. Every morning at 6 a.m., Nathan jumped on our bed and asked, "What time is it, Mum?" He seemed obsessed with time and said, "When are we going, Mum?" or, "When can my friends come over, Mum?" It was as if he knew he didn't have much time with us; that he needed to make every moment count. I was always trying to keep up with his energy, believing that if I kept him busy, he would eventually slow down. Sometimes I felt exhausted from his energy and some days he really tested my patience.

For Nathan's fifth birthday, we bought him *The Lion King* movie. It had been out for a few years and he loved it. He watched it over and over, and sang all the songs. It always surprised me how much he connected to it. His favorite part of the movie was watching the mean Uncle Scar sing with the hyenas, while he always grew quiet seeing Simba's father, Mufusa, die.

Although he was very active, Nathan could be shy with new people in new situations. After a few anxious tears, however, he settled into kindergarten and made friends easily. With all this high energy, Nathan would sometimes get into trouble wrestling with the other boys, but he was always repentant and it was easy to forgive him. His cute dimples and a sprinkle of freckles against his rosy cheeks always made me smile.

Nathan loved hugs and kisses, and never liked sleeping on his own. He always wanted company, which was difficult at times.

We had another child, a daughter, in 1995, when Nathan was three. He was very loving towards his sister, Lauren, but when he understood she was staying, he decided he needed more attention. Sometimes he squished her face and was a bit rough with her. He told us how cute she was, while really he was just trying to hurt her. Lauren made a wonderful difference in our lives and it wasn't long before Nathan fell in love with her too.

Nathan eventually took to his role as a big brother. He made his sister laugh as he tickled her or pulled funny faces. From a young age, Lauren loved her boisterous brother; her gentle nature accepted him as he was.

If Nathan ever got into trouble he said it was his tummy's fault. He would tell us, "My tummy doesn't want to go to sleep," or, "My tummy is too tired to clean up," or, "My tummy made me do it." He made us laugh as he told these stories and somehow he got away with it!

With all this energy, when Nathan was six, we decided to enroll him in rugby *and* taekwondo. Although he loved doing his sports, he became anxious when he was assessed in front of a lot of people. Once, when he was being graded for a new belt in taekwondo, he was particularly nervous. He asked several times that morning if he could miss the grading. We knew he could do it, and encouraged him to work through his fears and try. I felt sorry for him that day and wondered if we had made the right decision. We were proud as he stepped up and performed his routine in front of the crowd, showing us he had all the courage he needed to receive a new belt.

I started a journal for Nathan from the moment he was born. My dad wrote one for me and my two sisters, Sheryl and Lynn, and it was a tradition I wanted to carry on with my own children. We enjoyed reading about our childhood experiences, especially the funny things we said or did. The journal was a great way to record Nathan's funny comments or attitudes. One time when he asked for a drink, I said, "What's the magic word?" Instead of saying "please" he said, "Abracadabra." I often wrote about Nathan's busy energy. More importantly, however, I wrote about his kindness and love for everyone.

Trying to balance my work as a fitness teacher for high schools, and my time with Nathan and Lauren was difficult at times. Michael often travelled for his work as a sales manager and life was busy. On top of that, my parents lived interstate. My sister, Sheryl, lived nearby, however, and always supported me.

Nathan was happiest when he was playing with his friends or his cousins. He loved celebrating his birthday, and always pleaded for all of his friends to be there. He entertained everyone with his silly jokes and his infectious laugh.

Nathan loved going to school, although it wasn't to be the best student. He loved it because he enjoyed being with his friends, and while his attitude didn't always get him the best results, I understood over time, how important this was for him.

Nathan and Lauren were growing into beautiful, happy children. We had our difficulties like any normal family, and it was a busy time. Life was flying by. Nathan was already in grade four, and Lauren, who was turning six, had started her first year of school.

One night, as I was putting Nathan to bed, he said, "I don't ever want to get married."

This surprised me. I asked him, "Why?"

He answered with confidence, "Because that will mean I will be older, and that will mean I will die."

LOST IN TIME

❝ *You gain strength, courage, and confidence by every experience in which you really stop to look fear in the face. You are able to say to yourself, 'I have lived through this horror. I can take the next thing that comes along.' You must do the thing you think you cannot do.* **❞**
Eleanor Roosevelt

As I sat in the intensive care ward looking out the window on that winter's day in June 2001, I was amazed that life went on without me. Although nothing had changed for anyone else, I was there, praying that the doctors would save my son.

As we sat by Nathan's bedside, time stopped. There was only one other patient in the ward that day and the room felt cold and empty. The sound of the ventilator going up and down, in and out, helped me breathe slowly and lessened the symptoms of my anxiety.

Nathan was fully sedated and placed on life support, in the hope that his brain swelling would settle over a day or so. The results from the CAT scan were not good. He had crushed his skull and our only hope was to reduce the swelling.

I focused on every machine he was attached to, and watched for any slight changes or signs that he was responding. With tears in our eyes, each time a doctor or nurse came near us, we hoped for a positive diagnosis.

Besides a small cut on his leg, Nathan looked completely normal. There were no broken bones, stitches, or bruises. All the injuries were in his skull and brain stem. The brain stem controls the flow of messages between the brain and the rest of the body, and it controls basic body functions such as breathing, swallowing, heart rate, blood pressure, and consciousness.

After calling everyone with the devastating news, that night our extended family arrived from other parts of the country. They had managed to get flights in the evening. Michael picked up Lauren from Katrina's house so she could be with us.

It was comforting to have my sisters, Sheryl and Lynn, and both of our parents with us. Everyone was in shock. We prayed as we held his hand. The ICU became our home for the next few days. We roamed in shock, crying and comforting one another. Talking quietly with my dad on the first night, we tried to make sense of everything. But after a while, we both realized there were no words or explanations. Feeling his compassion and love in the silence was all I needed.

The next day, having survived on only a few minutes of sleep, I felt overwhelmed and anxious. A neurologist came in to test Nathan's brainwaves and breathing. In that particular test, they turned off his ventilator and waited for him to breathe on his own. The doctor said that if he failed to do this, he would be declared brain dead.

It took a few moments. It was agonizing to watch. I held my breath, too scared to let go. I was willing Nathan to fight harder and urging him to gasp for a breath. The silence was deafening, and, in the end, I could not look. The doctor reattached his ventilator. I felt numb, knowing what this meant.

That afternoon, more family and friends arrived. I was exhausted and I needed to turn some friends away. I found it difficult to find any extra energy. I needed every ounce I had for Nathan.

A few times I tried to sleep, but I kept shaking. The shock of the accident and the lack of sleep affected my whole body. We did not leave Nathan's side.

The next morning the neurologist returned and repeated the test. This time I did not watch at all, and I was too scared to know the truth.

Shortly afterwards, the head doctor of intensive care invited us into a private room. I remember her shutting the door, making the room feel smaller than it already was. From the look on her face, Michael and I knew deep down what she would say and yet, in those dark hours, we held onto any hope.

She looked tired as she gently explained to us the extent of the damage in his brain stem as a result of his skull being crushed on the road. She told us that we could keep him on life support if we wished, however, at some point, his heart would be overloaded and finally stop. She couldn't say when. She hesitated as she told us that the alternative was to say our last goodbyes that evening and donate his organs. We were shocked. We nodded in disbelief, too scared to open our mouths in case screams of agony escaped. Standing up to leave, I wondered how I would find the strength to share this news with family and friends. I wondered how anyone survived after hearing news like this.

We walked back to Nathan's bedside and we just wanted to shut the door, and shut out any more information about his impending death.

Shortly afterwards, we were surprised when three members of the organ donor team arrived. They asked us to fill out forms and make a quick decision about donating Nathan's organs. We struggled to find answers to their many questions. We asked to spend more time with Nathan, alone.

We held him and kissed his precious face as our tears overflowed. Questions flooded my mind. How could he be so vibrant and active just a day ago and now be on life support?

In our last moments with Nathan, I watched Michael hold him gently on his lap. It was heart-breaking. Seeing the pain and anguish on his face, knowing he was about to lose his son; it was too much to bear. Everything about this moment was surreal. We couldn't imagine our lives without him.

In the end, we knew Nathan would want to donate his organs, because he was such a generous boy. As soon as we told them our decision, he was placed on a trolley and taken down to surgery. I hugged and kissed him before they took him away. We felt detached from life and this situation. In that tragic moment, it was easier to pretend that he would return, healthy and happy.

Later that night, we were given a private room to use for our family and to lie with our son. This was our last chance to be with Nathan before we headed home the next day, without him. We put Lauren to sleep while we waited for Nathan to return from donating his organs. They brought Nathan to us on a trolley and Michael commented on how pale he looked. The nurse said to Michael, "You do know he's dead, don't you?" I tried to ignore her comment and the coldness of his cheek as I touched his face. My focus was only on Nathan, knowing this was our last time to be with him.

There were no decisions or thoughts about the future when I was holding my deceased child. Michael and I were exhausted, and lying next to Nathan felt normal. We kissed his forehead and spoke lovingly to him. I gently put my hand at the back of his head. The doctors had told us that he had crushed his skull and I wanted to feel it. I was shocked. His skull felt soft and caved in. It was broken into pieces. I wept silently. It didn't take long to fall asleep. I knew the moment was so precious, and so important. I never wanted to leave, knowing the pain ahead.

Early the next morning, while Lauren was still asleep in the room, the nursing staff came into our room with a black body bag. Even though we watched everything unfold, we were not registering our tragic reality. No one prepared us for the body bag and the nurses showed no emotion as they placed Nathan in it. As they zipped up the bag, his nose began to bleed. Everything inside of me wanted to wipe it. I wanted to scoop him up in my arms and take him back home where he belonged. I wanted to rip him out of that body bag and scream, "Stop it! Stop it! He is just a child!" Instead, we watched in silence, tears rolling down our cheeks.

I never imagined I would lose a child. In the devastation of this truth, I didn't believe anyone else could have felt this much pain and as my journey began without Nathan, it seemed impossible to believe that I could.

COURAGE

I never knew I had courage until I faced grief. Each day, I persuaded myself to keep going, one weary step at a time. Courage was a small voice within me that said, "Let go of today and start again tomorrow."

Coming home from the hospital with Lauren, but without Nathan, we were numb. The house was cold and empty. The silence was deafening. We walked into his room aching for his presence. We cried together, trying to comprehend our lives without him.

At first, I went on autopilot. It was impossible to absorb the implications of such an enormous shock. Nothing seemed real. Every limb in my body was heavy with grief. It was like walking through water—slow and difficult. When I look back, I am amazed how I coped.

Both Michael and I immediately went back to work. People were shocked by this and asked, "Should you be here?" I looked at them perplexed, wondering where they wanted us to go.

Of course, we knew we had to face the emotional pain ahead of us. We had a daughter to care for, and while everyone was running around trying to make us feel better, our grief was pushed into the background. We had no idea what *grieving* meant, and at the time, being busy was our best form of coping. We distracted ourselves by keeping our minds occupied with thoughts that weren't about Nathan. Family was staying with us at the time and this kept us busy. Friends were coming over regularly to offer support and even this helped us avoid the long term reality of losing our son.

After the funeral, and once our friends stopped coming around and the meals stopped being dropped by, Michael and I hoped we could continue to avoid our grief but eventually it started to surface. I began to accept the lack of sleep and the fog in my brain, but the ache in my heart for Nathan grew. Each day, my only hope was to be able to take another step.

Then one night, a few months after Nathan's death, I was out at a function. A friend and I were chatting about Nathan and the funny things he used to do. We were not talking for long but these memories triggered an overwhelming emotion in me. I felt it rise up and I knew I had to leave—I was hysterical and unable to control my sobs. The outburst surprised me and those around me, but of course it had nothing to do with what was said. Our conversation was a trigger for the bough to break, and for me to stop pretending that everything was fine.

At this time, Michael and I came out of shock and started piecing together exactly how this tragedy had happened to us. Even though we were told everything at the hospital, we started to question the information and our decision to turn off Nathan's life support.

We made an appointment with the head doctor of intensive care. She looked after Nathan while he was in hospital and we asked if we had made the right decision. Walking back into her office felt surreal. Once seated, we asked her, "Should we have turned off his life support? What if he came out of his coma after a few months?" Suddenly, we were plagued with doubt. The doctor looked at us sadly and assured us that Nathan would not have survived. She showed us his brain scans again and the extensive injuries to his brain stem. "Because of his injuries, he would not have been able to breathe on his own," she told us. She said that we made the right decision.

Michael and I looked at the x-rays a long time—black and white and grey—and still we could not comprehend that it was our Nathan. It could have been anyone's x-rays, and we felt no comfort in seeing them again or the fact she believed we had made the right decision. After the accident, he looked unharmed to us. All his injuries were hidden away inside his brain stem, and as much as the doctor tried to convince us, I found this hard to accept. We left the hospital that day, the truth of her words hovering over us like a dark cloud. We wanted to believe there was hope, that somehow we could resurrect him. I wanted to turn back the clock and start again and still hoped, deep down, this was possible. We arrived home, heavy with pain, unsure how to unravel our feelings and our illusions. And the silence between us grew.

Over the weeks following our consultation with Nathan's doctor, a flood of emotions consumed me with a deep anger at the center. At first, my anger was aimed at the driver. I wanted to punish her the same way our family had been punished. We enquired about whether she could be charged and held accountable for her actions. I wanted justice for her actions and I wanted her to feel my pain. With this built up anger, my energy was channeled in all the wrong directions, and I struggled to believe that Nathan was never coming home again. Sometimes, I imagined that he could walk through the door, and that life would return to normal again.

Days merged into months and my life felt like an emotional roller-coaster. Some days were easy and I could cope. Other days I felt alienated from everyone. On those days that I felt overwhelmed, I wanted to be alone. I didn't know how to deal with the heaviness of my emotions and I didn't want others to feel they had to fix me or listen to my problems. People meant well. They felt so awful that this had happened to us and I often sensed that their greatest fear was that it could happen to them.

Sometimes, people would try to tell me that they knew how I felt. They compared Nathan's death to losing a ninety year-old grandfather and it annoyed me. Disbelief crept into my awareness as I listened. So many people had a story about another death, and yet no one had lost a child. I felt alone and misunderstood.

In these early days, someone spoke to me and joked that she wished she could "run over" a friend who annoyed her. I looked at her in shock and wondered, *Have you forgotten how Nathan died?* At times, it seemed to me that people were insensitive to our grief. But the truth was that people didn't know what to do or say, and they felt unsure how to deal with this type of grief.

As time went on, I also started to play the 'what if' game. I would go over and over in my mind all the ways I could have avoided the accident. Once I let 'what if' in, it consumed me, and not only was I exhausted by my grief, but also by my busy mind. Often I would lie awake at night, trying to work out how I could have changed that tragic day. My mind was full of questions and I was overwhelmed with illusions of changing the day.

With all the busyness in my mind, I felt I needed to express myself. I wanted to talk with Michael about these thoughts but instead, Michael withdrew from talking about Nathan's death. I noticed that the worst time was when Michael arrived home from work. He was so sad and quiet. His silence was heavy, and at times like these, it built yet another wall of pain between us. It was difficult for me to understand the way Michael grieved. We had never grieved before, so it was new to both of us. I could see that I could not change the way he was grieving and yet, I wanted him to understand my way. I often talked to my family about my grief, which was a tremendous help. I was comforted by their support when I expressed my feelings with them and this diffused my anger. Knowing how much this connection strengthened me, it took time for me to accept Michael's way of grieving.

Connecting with people at this time often still proved difficult. Sometimes, friends and family thought I didn't want to talk about Nathan, because it might upset me. Other times, when I did talk about him, people felt uncomfortable when they realized how painful it was for me. The fact was, I never wanted to stop talking about Nathan simply because I knew he was never coming home. Sometimes people who meant well just made me feel worse. Comments like, "You are holding up so well" or "Time heals all wounds" or "Think of what you have to be thankful for" or "You have to be strong for others," were not helpful or constructive.

Sometimes in the early days, I just didn't have the energy or strength to cope with the grief of others, alongside the enormity of my own. When people came to my door and cried hysterically over their own experience of losing Nathan, I was overwhelmed, and sometimes I didn't know what to do with their feelings. I was grateful that Mum or my sister took turns answering the door. I also began to notice that I felt disappointed that the reactions of others did not fulfill my needs or meet my expectations. In fact, I didn't even know what my expectations were. I only wanted Nathan.

Life went on for nearly a year like this and it wasn't long before the anniversary of Nathan's death approached. I believed that if I prepared for it, I wouldn't collapse with grief on the day. What I found was, however, that grief never actually took hold of me on special occasions, but instead, it revealed itself when I least expected it. I was always surprised how grief overwhelmed me from the smallest triggers and how I felt there was no control over when that would happen.

I would remember him suddenly as I drove past a playground or when a song played on the radio from the *The Lion King*. Unfortunately, in those early years, I couldn't control when I felt vulnerable and emotionally exposed. It took years to adjust. I began to see that this sense of intense grief often happened when I was out socially. In the first stages of my grief, I felt a need to connect again with the life we had before Nathan died. I needed a sense of normalcy amongst the overwhelming feelings of grief. Part of me wanted to pretend that life could slip back to what it was like before, but every time I tried, it felt wrong. I made an effort to be stoic and show others that I was coping well, for their sake as well as my own, but this created tension inside me. At times, I noticed that no one mentioned Nathan's name and this made me feel worse. At social events, everyone talked about their sons and how well they were doing, confronting my reality even more. I wanted to join in and still talk about Nathan and his achievements. I wanted to say, "Remember when?" realizing, it was all I could say now.

EXPRESSIONS OF GRIEF

After the agony of losing Nathan, my grief endured. I dreaded the start of each new day, as it meant I had to face another twenty-four hours without Nathan. Grief affected every part of my life and it came in unpredictable waves. It affected my thoughts and changed the way I saw the world. At times, it compromised my energy and health. Over time, I began to understand that grief would stay.

When Nathan died, I lost my hopes, dreams, and expectations for his future. In essence, a part of me died with him as well. Over time, I discovered ways that allowed me to nurture these feelings of loss. I came to recognize the devastation of Nathan's death expressed itself in many ways, and I discovered strategies to work through these feelings.

Expressions of Grief and Strategies That Helped

- *Withdrawing Socially*—this happened not long after Nathan died. The energy it took to grieve was enormous, and normal social events became overwhelming. I felt like I could no longer control my emotions. I felt exposed and vulnerable in every conversation. I became aware I needed to step back and nurture myself during this period.

- *Having Trouble Thinking or Concentrating*—my emotions took over my mind on occasion. At times, I focused only on my loss. Although there were days of clarity and normalcy, concentrating was difficult for me. This was temporary and over time, it lifted.

- *Lack of Appetite*—in the beginning of my grieving, I felt deflated. Food, wine, and cooking no longer interested me. I lost my zest for life. How could I enjoy anything again without Nathan? Everything I used to enjoy had lost its meaning.

- *Dreams*—the first dream I had of Nathan was after a yoga class. Dreams of my son were precious. I woke up feeling like we had just been together and I longed for any moment that made me feel like that. Not everyone dreams. I wrote my dreams down in a journal so I could remember them.

- *Insomnia*—in the first few weeks, it was very difficult to sleep. If I did, I would sometimes have a nightmare about the accident. There was so much going on in my mind. I would struggle to relax and let go. It took time to settle into a normal sleep pattern. Having naps during the day helped me catch up.

- *Becoming Preoccupied with Death or Events Surrounding Death*—this happened a lot in the first few months. I was often preoccupied with knowing about other deaths. In September 2001, a few months after Nathan's death, 9/11 occurred. I felt connected to tragedy. I knew what they were feeling. I knew the face of death.

- *Searching for Reasons*—finding meaning after Nathan died was extremely important to me. I began my search early on. I read many books on death and how to heal. I wanted a reason for his death. I wanted to find a purpose for my own life after this immense loss.

- *Dwelling on Mistakes, Real or Imagined*—this was a big burden for me. I felt so much guilt in the beginning. I was overwhelmed at times, remembering only what I didn't do for him. I dwelled on what we could have or should have done and I felt like I had so much to say to him.

- *Feeling Alone and Distant from others*—this was very true in the beginning. No one I knew had ever lost a child, and I felt alone. Because no one understood how I felt, I felt disconnected from them. Spending time away from others and finding a sense of solitude helped me come to terms with my feelings and helped me nurture my needs and take small steps.

- *Crying Frequently*—every song or reminder of Nathan made me cry. I slowly adjusted to these emotions. I never used to cry easily, so this was new for me. Nathan's loss opened the flood gates.

- *Anger, Guilt and Blame*—I was very angry at the driver who hit Nathan. After the accident, I wanted to blame and seek justice for his death. I felt overwhelmed with emotions and wanted the driver to feel remorse and guilt.

- *Physical Health (Headaches, Lowered Immune System)*— I had lots of coughs and colds in the first year. I had a lot of headaches too. My emotions clouded my mind and the stress of grief lowered my immune system. I soon learned I needed to slow down and be present with my feelings.

- *Tension or Problems with Personal Relationships*—a few months after losing Nathan, I noticed I was grieving differently to Michael. I was outwardly grieving while Michael internalized it. I also became aware that his family and my family were grieving differently too. At first, I really struggled with this. It was hard to understand the difference. Over time and with patience, we adjusted.

- *Loss of Meaning and Identity*—I had moments when I felt overwhelmed with the injustice of his death and struggled with questions like, *How could this have happened to us? Why did Nathan deserve to die? How will I go on without him my life? Who am I, if I am not his mother?*

At first, I wasn't sure how to cope with all my emotions. I felt lost in my thoughts and wanted to connect with others who felt the same. As a counselor and a mother, I began to understand how important it was to express my grief and feel heard. Sometimes our family and friends were overwhelmed by our emotions and uncertain how to support us. After a few months of this, both Michael and I decided to see a psychologist. The psychologist had an unbiased perspective of my grief, and it was good to be able to share my feelings and know she would not feel overwhelmed by them. We both felt comfortable speaking and sharing in that environment. There are many counselors and psychologists to choose from, and we knew that finding the right match for us was important. Michael and I both understood that we needed someone experienced in sudden, unexpected grief, and even more specifically, someone who understood the complex loss of a child.

We also attended *The Compassionate Friends Support Network*, which is part of a world-wide non-profit organization offering friendship, understanding, grief education, and hope to families following the death of a son or daughter. All bereaved parents, grandparents, and siblings are welcomed. Michael and I attended a meeting for grieving parents about six months after Nathan died. Still raw in our grief, we were searching for answers. We thought it would help to be with like-minded parents. We felt very welcomed on the night. There were around six parents waiting when we arrived and we were asked to sit down. The chairs were set out in a circle. Each of us was asked to share the story of how we lost our child. The first person to speak was a mother. She was clearly distraught and emotional. She began by sharing about her twenty year old son who had committed suicide. As she struggled to get the words out, I felt my emotions rise up with hers. It was her next sentence that shocked me the most. She explained that it had been fifteen years since it happened. The sharing continued around the circle. No one had recently lost a child and yet, everyone was crying and highly emotional. By the time Michael and I came to share, we felt overwhelmed with *their* grief. I felt concerned that perhaps I would never feel hope.

Compassionate friends around the world have many support systems in place and it is important to find the group for you and also the right timing. Michael and I felt comfort knowing that we were not alone, and that if we ever needed support from a counselor, psychologist, or a parent's network, it was available anytime. We also felt more determined than ever to find our way through this pain. We understood then that this journey was ours to create, as well as endure, and no one could do that for us.

REMEMBERING

"After death, memories are all I have, each one more precious with time."
Karen Lang

After the funeral, the visitors, our families visiting, and the meals arriving, I still wanted to talk about Nathan and the grief I was experiencing.

In Western society, many people tend to forget quickly about the pain and intensity of grief others are experiencing; and often, people cannot understand the enormity of a child's death. I saw that it was difficult for others to understand my fears and the wildly fluctuating emotions I was experiencing. In conversation, some people tried to change the subject or make light of my grief. I understood that Nathan's death made them uncomfortable and unsure of what to say, but it didn't make it any easier for me. I didn't have the strength to work with my emotions and then teach others as well.

Often, friends or family worried that they would offend me. They really wanted to support us and wanted to know how they could help as they were as new to this as I was. This took patience and understanding on both sides, and with courage, I learned to express my feelings more openly. Sometimes, I gently reminded others that it helped when they listened or that I appreciated their interest in my journey. And sometimes, I had to accept that no one would ever really understand what I felt; something I learned to do a little more easily with the benefit of time.

Encouraging others to know what I needed was difficult for me. At first, it didn't help that I didn't even know what I wanted and hoped that everyone else knew. They didn't. This was frustrating. Finding the strength, and even just the words, to express to others what I wanted, added to my long 'to do' list of grief. When I understood what I needed, I then found the courage to ask. It then became easier for me and for my support network. With the death of our child, we were forced to do the impossible—to build a new life and discover a new normal for ourselves and our families in a world that no longer included our child.

What I Needed From My Friends and Family

- I wanted to be able to talk freely about Nathan and his life.
- I wanted others to listen and allow me to express my emotions, without offering a quick fix or trying to solve my problems.
- I sometimes needed time alone, and I didn't want my friends to make a fuss or worry because I was doing this.
- It took time for me to accept that some family members did not feel comfortable speaking about Nathan or his death.
- I wanted family and friends to remember Nathan's birthday and anniversary, especially in the first few years. This meant a lot to me.

- I did not want to feel overwhelmed with other people's grief. I was already overwhelmed with my own.

Suggestions for Family and Friends

- I learned that it was often difficult for friends and family to know what to say or do when we were grieving. They were afraid of intruding, saying the wrong thing, or making us feel even worse.
- I was grateful when our friends and family called us and asked us how we were doing. It was comforting to know that they were there for us. More than ever, their support was needed during this time. They did not always know exactly what to say or what to do, but that was okay, they didn't need to know the answers or give advice. Good listeners and support were well-received.
- I appreciated the fact that the people we knew felt overwhelmed with their own grief at times and sought out another friend or a trained counselor to sift through their grief. We found sudden outpourings of grief overwhelming and compromised our energy.
- While I never wanted to be forced to open up, I appreciated knowing I had permission to talk about my loss.
- I appreciated when people spoke openly about Nathan and didn't steer away from the subject when his name came up. When it was appropriate, some people asked sensitive questions that invited me to openly express my feelings, even just, "Do you feel like talking?"
- Like many people, I needed to tell my story over and over again, sometimes in minute detail and so patience was needed

from those around me. Repeating the story is a way of
processing and accepting the death.

- The most important thing that our grieving friends and
family did was to simply be there. Their support and caring
presence helped quell the pain so we could begin to heal.

Practical Ways to Help

- Shop for food or run errands
- Drop off a meal or other type of food
- Listen and support them
- A gentle hug
- Help with the funeral arrangements
- Offer to help take phone calls and receive guests
- Take care of some housework, such as cleaning or laundry
- Watch the children or pick them up from school
- Help with pets, if they have them
- Go with them to support meetings
- Accompany them on a walk
- Take them to lunch or a movie

These are examples of how I expressed my grief to others
and how I accepted help. They also show how friends and family
were supportive. I found that most people really did want to
support us during this time and cared deeply about our journey;
sometimes, they just needed a little guidance in learning how.

SUPPORT

*" We can live without religion
and meditation, but we cannot
survive without human affection. "*
Dalai Lama

I have always struggled with receiving help from friends, but after Nathan died, I had to learn to accept support from others. At first, I believed it was easier to protect myself from receiving so I did not have to reveal my vulnerability to others. Over time, I understood that acting stoic while experiencing immense grief was not beneficial to anyone.

Although we were only at the hospital for two days after the accident, we received wonderful support from family, friends, and staff, so that we could be completely absorbed with Nathan. We did not focus on anything outside of the hospital; nothing else mattered. My mother and father, two sisters, and Michael's family were by our side from the beginning and friends came up to the hospital with toiletries, food, or anything we asked for. There were lots of hugs and tears. Our beautiful friends offered us love and support and this kept us going through those difficult days. In the first month, almost everyone we knew wanted to help in some way. When we arrived home, we were exhausted and making decisions about anything was extremely difficult. Our family, close friends, and church community gave us immense support, especially in planning Nathan's funeral, which was a beautiful expression of this support all around us. We felt embraced by our community in our time of need.

After the funeral, we didn't feel like leaving the house. Even daily chores like shopping or attending appointments were overwhelming. I didn't want to bump into people who did not know about the accident, or even those who asked, "How's everything going?" Having to take Lauren to Nathan's old school was difficult. At first, everyone stared at us and we sensed how much this affected the whole community. When they did approach us with support, it was tainted with sadness. Our school was the last place everyone had seen Nathan.

Over time, I activated new thoughts and allowed my family, friends, and members of my community to know what I needed. I accepted when people offered to prepare family meals or take care of Lauren. I allowed myself to use this time to eat, sleep, and rest as much as I needed. Below are some ways I accepted support that was offered to us and this really helped me cope each day.

Ways to Accept Support

- *Say Yes to Meals and Support for the Funeral*—we had so many wonderful people support us. Meals were dropped off every day. This helped us focus on our emotions and resting and gave us time to be together as a family.
- *Accept Help to Look After Other Children*—going up to the school to get Lauren was difficult. Facing everyone seemed

to increase my grief. Having friends drop Lauren home or take her to activities at times really helped.

- *Allow Time for Rest*—because I didn't sleep well in the beginning, I needed to rest during the day. I became exhausted by visitors and having to make decisions about the future. My mum often turned away visitors when this happened. Each time I nurtured myself, I felt stronger.

- *Start a Journal*—I started a journal and wrote down my thoughts and feelings. I used this time to be in a place where I could express my emotions and let them go. I focused on my gratitude for the support and love I was receiving and wrote them in my journal.

- *Have a Massage, Pedicure, or Facial to Relax*—I have always felt guilt about making time for me. I found that massage was a wonderful way to release the tension and stress that grief caused. Each time I slowed down, I began to accept my feelings and nurture my pain.

- *Say Yes to Outside Support*—It's comforting to know that if I ever needed extra support, or a different perspective, I could make time to see a counselor or a psychologist. When I felt nurtured, I was able to nurture Lauren and Michael. This made all the difference in our healing together, and helped me stay present with them.

LAUREN

" If tears could build a
stairway and thoughts a memory
lane; I'd walk right up to heaven
and bring you home again. "
Unknown

O ur daughter Lauren was five years old when Nathan
died. Waiting in the intensive care unit, one of the
psychologists asked where our daughter was. We told
her she was with Katrina, our good friend, who was taking
care of her. She gently suggested that it was important for her
to be here with us, considering the seriousness of Nathan's
injuries. Having Lauren with us helped her begin processing
her brother's death. It gave her a chance to see the situation first
hand, rather than imagine it. It gave her an opportunity to say
her last goodbyes to Nathan before the funeral.

It wasn't until she arrived at the hospital that I could see how
important it was. I am so glad we were guided that day. In our
shock and grief, we couldn't think straight or make decisions
that might affect us later. As parents, we must be sensitive to
our other children and their feelings, letting them know what

is happening during this difficult time. Expressing our heartfelt emotions and sadness with them is important too, as it allows them to express their emotions as well. Lauren was with us while all the decisions about Nathan were made. I felt it gave her a sense of belonging, and although it was painful and sad, she was able to be with her brother until the end. She didn't do or say much at the hospital. She too was in shock and was trying to absorb such a tragic event. The psychologist took her a couple of times to draw pictures and just be a normal child. Still, we were all there together, and we did our best to get through this difficult time.

When we arrived home from the hospital, Lauren was very detached and sad. Often I would look over at her and see a part of her had died too. This caused me great concern as I understood my responsibility for her grief as well. It was important that we allowed Lauren to grieve in her own way. Being so young, she did not fully understand that this new situation was permanent and this aspect was part of her grief as well. She was still in shock, like we were, and was trying to process this immense loss.

Every day was different, and although we were overwhelmed with our own grief, we knew Lauren needed our love, attention, and support. We included Lauren as best we could to help her transition through these times, and we were guided by those around us to help her understand her own grief and Nathan's death.

- *Be Honest*—I found it was best to present the information in a straightforward manner with age-appropriate information by explaining the situation clearly—Nathan died last night after the accident. Avoid vague answers—he went to sleep or he's gone away. These terms leave children wondering if they will die when they go to sleep or if the person is coming back.

- *Don't Delay*—delaying a gentle, age-appropriate talk about death can do more harm than good. I understood that if I waited, someone else might tell Lauren. I wanted her to hear it from Michael and I. Alternatively, I knew she might overhear something in conversation. Learning the news from us was less frightening.

- *Answer Questions*—some children are satisfied with the facts. Others will ask a multitude of questions. I allowed questions, and answered them as best as I could, admitting when I didn't have the answer.

- *Recognize Fears*—death is a scary concept for children. Michael and I decided that if Lauren expressed any fear about seeing Nathan's body or going to the funeral, we would not force the issue, however, she did not do this. Comfort and reassurance took precedence as we helped her through her fears and allowed them to be expressed. We felt that when Lauren felt safe with us, she was able to express her feelings and fears, and this way her fears did not build up into anxiety or stress.

- *Accepting Grief*—I let Lauren see me cry and believed that when I openly expressed my emotions, I allowed her to feel free to show hers. I wanted her to feel comfortable showing me these emotions but I had to teach her by example first. Emotional pain and expressing it is part of losing a loved one.

- *Cherish the Memories*—I talked about Nathan and my love for him, gently inviting Lauren to do the same if she wished. We looked through photo albums, talked about funny things he used to do, and the special memories we had with him.

A few months after Nathan's death, I read a book about how children can blame themselves for their sibling's death and can carry tremendous guilt. Often children do not share this information out of fear of repercussions. I was concerned after reading this, and went into Lauren's room and gently asked her whether she felt any guilt about Nathan's death. I was shocked when she answered, "Yes."

She told me when Nathan received his *Dragonball Z* cards on the day of the accident, she was jealous. She said she felt angry at him and wished he would die. I never imagined this is what she would say, and I certainly did not know she was carrying this burden. That night was a perfect opportunity to listen and understand how she felt. When I took the time to discuss this with her, I was able to free her from the guilt she was carrying. This allowed her to hear the truth that she was not responsible in any way.

I think it's easy to underestimate how much children take in during a tragedy or death and how aware they are in a difficult situation. There is a trap in believing that parents can protect children from the truth by not discussing the tragedy with them. Left to themselves, children have a tendency to create their own story about a sibling's death, creating deeper issues of guilt and fear.

Nathan's death changed Lauren's life forever, and her ability to adapt and understand grief was our responsibility. As a family, we had to work together and be there for each other. As we supported one another, we were surprised by what she had to say. Lauren showed wisdom and a capacity to comfort us in times of despair. One night, when I was putting Lauren to bed, I started to cry and said, "I just want Nathan to come home."

She looked at me for a few moments before she replied confidently, "But Mummy, he is home."

Strategies That Helped

- We made time to be with Lauren as we grieved, knowing fully that she was grieving too. Most importantly, we understood that she wanted to be heard, just like we did. We used activities that were appropriate for her age, like playing or going out for a treat and an opportunity to connect. These were times to listen and ask questions about how she was feeling.
- Our time with the psychologist in the hospital was extremely valuable. Understanding what Lauren needed in those dark days helped guide us. I felt empowered when I knew how to help Lauren through her stages of grief.
- We read age-appropriate stories together about grief and discussed how the children in the story coped after a death in their families. This helped identify some of the feelings Lauren was experiencing and helped her express her concerns and questions. Some of those stories included:
  - *A Taste of Blackberries* by D. B. Smith (2004)
  - *Beat the Turtle Drum* by C. Greene (1976)
  - *If Nathan Were Here* by Mary Bahr (2000)
  - *A Memory Book: Someone I Love Has Died* by Tricia Irving and Bev Gatenby (2000)
  - *The Sky Dreamer* by Anne Morgan and Celine Eimann (2010)
  - *Bridge to Terabithia* by Katherine Paterson *(1977)*

- Creating a memory box gave us a physical place to go to and look at items that reminded us of the special memories and times that we had together.
- Drawing pictures is a powerful form of art therapy. Lauren loved drawing, and this was a perfect expression of her feelings and having time to be creative with her grief.
- Writing down questions Lauren might have had for Nathan and imagining how he might respond was another way to foster a healing discussion. Lauren had lots of questions about Nathan like, "Where is he now?" or "Is he coming back soon?" This activity gave her a chance to clear up her fears and doubts about his death.
- Meditation or simple breathing exercises are also valuable tools for children. *Enchanted Meditations for Kids* by Christiane Kerr is an audio CD suitable for children up to twelve years.

GRIEVING DIFFERENTLY

❝ In this sad world of ours, sorrow comes to all, and it often comes with bitter agony. Perfect relief is not possible except with time. You cannot now believe that you will ever feel better. But this is not true. You are sure to be happy again. ❞
Abraham Lincoln

One of the more difficult situations that Michael and I discovered along this journey was how differently we expressed our grief. During the initial period of the overwhelming shock, it didn't occur to either of us that this would be a problem. It was a few months later that I noticed it. My personality type is naturally expressive and I found it easy to share my pain and sadness about Nathan's death. I felt lighter when I was able to express my grief with others, whereas Michael found this very difficult. He would come home from work extremely sad and quiet. Dinner at the table each night was silent and heavy. I encouraged him to talk about his pain, but it was too difficult for him and this caused us to feel disconnected from one another. At the time, I was frustrated by his silence and his way of grieving. I wanted him to open up to me.

Around this time, however, I began to read about grief and learned how we all grieve differently. I became aware that neither of us was grieving the right way, just in our own way. This understanding didn't make it any easier in the first year but it gave me insight into this issue. With time, I understood that his deep pain and loss was exactly like mine—he just expressed it in a different way. He protected his feelings about Nathan because they were so important to him. Sometimes Michael went out with his friends and shared his feelings, but he found it difficult because a lot of men felt it was too challenging to speak about grief. He often came home from these nights wishing that his friends could understand the depth of his pain.

As a counselor, I have seen how quickly grief strains a relationship, leaving both partners feeling disconnected and stuck. Shutting down emotions is a way people protect themselves from intense pain, and although this may help for a little while, loved ones eventually feel alienated and locked out. As I learned to accept the way Michael expressed his sadness, I found I could see a way through. I spent more time focusing on my grief and how I could heal my pain, rather than trying to help Michael change the way he grieved. This approach slowly helped us both, allowing us to create more space for love and connection.

Strategies That Helped Me Bridge the Gap with Others Who Were Grieving

- I allowed myself time alone in nature. This helped me balance my thoughts and release my stress. It also gave me clarity and energy to work through these changes.
- Allowing others to express their pain in their own ways was helpful. Some people prefer to write instead of talk, some prefer to draw or paint instead of cry.

- When I did not understand how someone was grieving, I tried to make time to sit together and share the ways we felt comfortable grieving. In this way, we helped each other process our grief.
- When I felt that Michael was completely closed off, I tried to let him be. I came to understand that I could not heal the wounds of others. It was up to each person to heal and to do it when they were ready.
- When I felt that I could not express my grief freely with Michael, but I really needed to talk, I called on friends or family who were able to listen and support me.

Grief has taught me that everyone needs to find his or her own way of releasing emotional pain. As I improved my ability to accept and love myself, I found that I allowed others to heal in their own way and in their own time.

GRIEF—A NEW GUEST

"This being human is a guest house. Every morning is a new arrival. A joy, a depression, a meanness, some momentary awareness comes as an unexpected visitor. Welcome and entertain them all. Treat each guest honorably. The dark thought, the shame, the malice, meet them at the door laughing, and invite them in. Be grateful for whoever comes, because each has been sent as a guide from beyond."

Rumi

When I began grieving, my emotions felt like new guests arriving each day, and I wasn't sure who would be there when I woke up. Sometimes it was anger or fear. Some days it was overwhelming sadness. Sometimes I didn't answer the door at all, and yet the more I ignored these guests, the more they kept coming around. Slowly, I adapted to the expectation that there would always be someone new to invite in. At times, there were too many emotional visitors to cope with, and on these days, I retreated, hoping they would go away.

Over time, as I became more aware of the power of my thoughts, I would peek out to see who was at my door. Each time a new guest arrived, I grew more accustomed to inviting them in. I began to see that when I invited them in and sat with these guests, I became better at accepting them. Some came and left quickly, and others stayed a while. Regardless, it wasn't easy. Although I had adapted to my difficult visitors, I hoped it would not always be this way; but as time passed, I understood that it was grief that invited these visitors to my door. I also became aware that, eventually, the difficult guests stopped coming around so often; and I began to notice a shift. New guests started to arrive. Some days it was peace, and other days it was relief. Sometimes, it was awareness and happiness. I also noticed that around Nathan's birthday, the difficult guests would turn up again. The difference this time was that I remembered them and I knew that, after a while, they would leave. This went on for many years and, as I embraced these guests, I found that the ones I loved would stay more often.

A Meditation for Acceptance

Sit quietly

Take some deep breaths

Who is at the door today?

Is the door closing or opening to this feeling?

What would happen if I opened the door? What would happen if I invited this feeling in?

Can I sit with these feelings for a while to see what they have to say? Can I embrace this feeling without judgment?

Finish the stillness with some deep, releasing breaths

Some of my emotional guests still make me feel uncomfortable, but I allow them in. I accept that they have arrived to teach me, or challenge me to let go of any number of aspects or themes in my life. They may be asking me to let go of my control over some part of my life. It can be to let go of a fear that I am holding. It can be to allow myself to receive a gift of support or love. When I understand why they are here, these guests do not stay as long. I found that they are here to remind me who I am; and who I can become.

ANNIVERSARIES

O n Nathan's anniversary each year, we celebrate his life by creating a special event. Of course it was tainted with immense grief in the first few years but as time passed, we began to understand that planning something special for this day helped us handle our grief. In the early years, it was a simpler event. We went to his grave every birthday and anniversary. We took plants or balloons, and placed them at his graveside. On the same day, we would go out to lunch or dinner, and honor his life and our time with him. Later on that same day, we would also play old videos of him growing up. Sometimes we would watch a DVD that he used to love. In those moments, there were always lots of tears but it was good to release these feelings together as a family. We wanted to remember the special years we shared with Nathan, and this helped us heal.

It was always a sad day but recalling wonderful memories and the happiness we shared helped connect us to him. At times, the day was filled with emotions but for some reason, the anticipation of the day was worse than the day itself. Sometimes on the day, I felt anxious, sad or angry. Other times, I relived every moment of the day and his death, and those days were the hardest. When I allowed my emotions to be felt, however, it helped release my heaviness. When I learned to verbalize my needs, desires or wishes, I found that most people were happy to support me, and it helped to remind them about his anniversary or birthday. In the end, I was glad I did.

On Nathan's anniversary in the early days, we never made it a big event. We only invited immediate family and maybe a few friends who were sensitive to our grief. Having a lot of people fussing over me made it more difficult, and I learned to nurture my needs and do what was right for my family.

I found it helpful to learn about other cultures and how they expressed their grief and celebrated the life of their loved ones. In Jewish culture, they observe yahrzeit on the anniversary of a loved one's death. Yahrzeit observance begins at night when a 24 hour candle is lit, and as one woman describes it, "The spirit of the dead person fills the room again for 24 hours." We light Nathan's baptismal candle on the day of his anniversary every year.

In Mexico, people are more culturally familiar with death and are not afraid to speak of it; death is never hidden away. The Day of the Dead, or *Dia de los Muertos*, is a Mexican holiday celebrated annually on the 1st of November throughout Mexico—in particular, the Central and South regions, and it is acknowledged around the world in other cultures. The holiday focuses on gatherings of family and friends to pray for and even celebrate friends and family members who have died, as a way to help support their spiritual journey. I knew I never wanted to forget Nathan either and wanted to honor his life in a similar way.

Ideas We Used For Nathan's Anniversary

- Planning a special dinner or lunch with close friends helped us celebrate his life and connect with our families. It gave us a time and place to gather and remember him as a family and gave us a chance to grieve, but more importantly, to honor Nathan.
- Asking those who came to bring a photo of our child and share a story or memory invited a special kind of participation. We did this with Lauren and this helped her share her memories about Nathan and her grief.
- On special occasions we take a plant, a toy, or balloons to his grave.
- Creating a quilt with pictures of your child is also a beautiful project.
- Nathan's school made a plaque and placed it in the playground. The plaque can include a name and perhaps a quote or favorite saying.
- Cooking Nathan's favorite meal or eating at his favorite restaurant was a way to bring us together. Nathan loved spaghetti or fish and chips and we would create meals he loved.
- I received a beautiful piece of jewelry from some special friends who engraved all my children's names on the back. This was lovely to wear and to hold, reminding me that I had three children.

- Creating a memory box full of special items that Nathan loved gave us another place where we could remember him or leave notes to him. Ours contained Nathan's *Dragon Ball Z* cards, his drawings, and awards he had received.
- Planting a tree or a bush or a flower garden in memory of a child is a lasting gift that embraces life. Our local council created a beautiful resting place in the street where Nathan died. It is special to us and we feel honored there is one for him.

Reminders aren't just tied to the calendar. Sometimes my triggers were tied to sights, sounds and smells—and they overwhelmed me when I least expected it. The sound of any loud noise took me back to the accident scene. Sometimes seeing Nathan's friends look sad or lost without him saddened me. Even memorial celebrations for others triggered the pain of my loss.

Life would never be the same again, no matter how much I wanted it to be. However, focusing on the positive memories and positive times I had with Nathan helped me let go of my guilt, pain, and sadness. When I only remembered what I didn't do, when I only remembered that his life was cut short, I lost sight of the gift he gave me while he was here.

I Remember
by Michael Lang

Today I remember our son
I remember his smile, his cheeky grin
I remember his energy, his desire to always be on
the run
I remember your love for him and my drive for him
I remember our focus and our plans for him
I remember

SIGNS

Before Nathan died, I never looked for signs in my life. If life wasn't flowing, I just accepted it. When I felt uneasy about something, I took no steps to change my direction. I never believed I had power to listen or connect to the flow and synchronicity of life.

At the beginning of the year, before Nathan's death, we put our house on the market. In retrospect, I can see there were clear signs not to sell our home at that time, even the real estate agent did not want to sell it. We experienced resistance on every level and yet, I continued to push.

When I became aware that life was showing me signs, I learned to read them. Over time, this has helped guide me to make the right decisions, in the right time. Signs are everywhere, and as I practiced stillness, I connected to a flow of energy, and as so many traditions, religions, and wise sages have been teaching over the centuries, I understood that I was connected to everything.

When I trained my heart to listen, and my eyes to see, I became more aware. I learned to listen and notice the *little miracles* that popped up each day and I began to see special messages, just waiting for me to open them.

Remembering back to the day before Nathan died, when he had pleaded with me to take that day off school, I realized that this was a sign. It was signaling me to tell me to stop, listen and spend time with him. He asked me again that night, and again I said, "No."

Looking back, these signs were very clear, and once I saw them for what they were, I developed a deep sense of guilt. Finding a way to forgive myself for not slowing down would prove extremely difficult.

Early in my grief, I read a book by Dr Elisabeth Kübler-Ross MD, *On Children and Death,* where she writes about her experience with parents in bereaved workshops who have lost a child. She discovered that many of these parents found indications of their child's inner awareness of their impending death. Some children left a spontaneous drawing or art as a sign before they died. At first, I thought it seemed impossible that Nathan knew of his impending death, however as I continued to read her book, I was fascinated by the stories shared by these parents and the messages their children had left for them. I started to think that maybe Nathan might have left a sign for us. I put down the book and went straight into his room. Only a few moments later, I found the first sign. My heart skipped a beat as I saw a folder on his desk. I opened it. On one side of the folder was a drawing of a cloud. Inside the cloud it read: 'Natty in heaven'. I stood there in shock.

The next sign was a drawing I found in my diary. It was of a parked car on the road with the door open. There was pen scribbled all around the curb on the road. The day that Nathan was hit by the car, my car door was open, and Nathan's head hit the curb.

I showed these pictures to Michael immediately and he was just as shocked as I was. We had so many questions about these drawings. The next sign we found was in Nathan's science book from school. This particular drawing confronted us the most. Nathan had drawn a car which looked like an ambulance and above this was an angel flying. It read: 'Heaven'. Next to the car, he had drawn an arrow that pointed to the exact spot where his head hit the edge of the curb. This was where he landed when he was hit by the car. Below that picture and on the same page was a gravestone that read: 'Kill Cars'. The cars were headed in the same direction as the accident.

Drawn by Nathan Lang (April 2001)

My heart sank as I took in all this information. My mind raced with thoughts, wondering, *How did he know?* He never spoke of it, and he never showed us these drawings.

Parents from around the world have shared stories about the signs their child left for them. It seems the younger children leave signs and messages in the form of drawings or art, while older children might leave a poem or a letter. There doesn't seem to be any sense of fear, in what they speak of or draw, particularly regarding their deaths. Some children have told their parents, "I am going to be with Jesus today."

Their parents will sometimes reply, "That's nice dear," or "No, darling, you only go to heaven when you die."

Two nights before Nathan died, I found him in his room, reading the Bible. I did find this surprising but I didn't say anything to him. I guess I was caught up in the moment watching him look so peaceful.

While we may never fully understand why children leave signs, Michael and I were comforted by Nathan's drawings. I truly believe he left them for us. They helped us understand that on the day of his tragic death, I was never in control. It was his time to leave us and it was always going to happen. We all have our own beliefs about signs but sometimes there are none. Still, over time, people shared their experiences with me of witnessing a sign, after their loved one has died. In a special moment, when they were remembering or honoring their child, a butterfly, a bird, or an animal appeared.

After Nathan died, we seemed to attract butterflies. They were always around his grave and when they landed near us, we liked to think Nathan was near us too. These signs along our journey were for us to discover. And we just knew in our hearts when they came.

Strategies to Connect to Signs

- *Slowing Down*—I had to learn how to slow down and listen. When I was busy in my mind and my life, I didn't notice these signs and I didn't see the universe was trying to speak to me. This is where meditation and yoga has helped guide me and connect me more deeply to the synchronicity and mystery of life.

- *Pay Attention*—I began to pay attention to everything I was doing. I began to practice mindfulness. Being aware of my thoughts, the environment I was in, and the people around me encouraged me to grow. Sometimes I felt the signs were clear, like signs on the road. But I came to see that if I didn't look, I might miss them. I noticed that friends or family would share an idea with me, which gave me deeper insight. When I trained myself to listen, answers were given. Sometimes, even a complete stranger gave me a sign through a word or a gesture. These moments reassured me that I was on the right path.

- *Animals are Teachers too*—every time an animal grabs my attention, I look and listen. Sometimes, it was an owl, a kookaburra or a butterfly. They all reminded me of something or taught me another of life's valuable lessons. When a specific animal kept returning, I looked up the meaning of that animal to understand and be guided by the message it has for you. There are many sources, such as *Medicine Cards* by Jamie Sams and *Animal Speak* by Ted Andrews, which draw upon ancient traditions and indigenous wisdom to trace the roots of an animal's appearance in our lives.

- *Flow and Resistance*—for me, this is the most powerful sign. Anytime my life is not flowing easily, I step back and re-evaluate my situation and my decisions. Resistance appears in our lives for a reason, and it is a way we can understand our lives on a deeper, more resonant and complete level. Sometimes I have found resistance because I am not allowing or trusting in life's contours. Sometimes it is because I am impatient and believe I know better. No matter what, the signs are there for us to read and when we do, we allow the synchronicity and abundance of life to flow more easily towards us.

LETTING GO

> *"To hold, you must first open your hand. Let go."*
> *Lao Tzu*

In 2002, after ten years in our family home and one year living without Nathan, I discovered I was pregnant with my third child. We had been trying to sell our house before Nathan died and once we found out I was pregnant, this solidified our decision to buy a new home and rent our house out. It still wasn't a good market to sell in and so we decided to rent it out for a year. This decision was not taken lightly. All my memories of Nathan and Lauren's childhood were there. It was very special to us.

Moving and beginning again, as difficult as it was, allowed me to move into another phase of my grief. I realized in my sadness that all of my memories were locked inside my heart. No one could ever take them from me, they would not be left behind in a move and they would never be lost. It was also a difficult but good opportunity to let go of some of Nathan's toys, clothes, and books. I have heard some people say they are reluctant to let go, as if these material things are all they have left of their children, and they are afraid they are losing their only connection to them, but I felt it was an opportunity to lighten my grief. For me, it was time.

Letting go and moving did not leave my grief and pain behind, but it did give me the courage to know that I could leave our family home, let go of some of his personal items, and still feel close to him. We gave his clothes and toys to friends or family, and this helped us feel better about parting with them. Letting go didn't mean I forgot Nathan or the precious memories we shared. It meant I no longer held onto that time. I understood that staying there because of guilt or of fear was not living in the present.

The move was sad. I never believed I could let go of another layer of my grief, but I did, and each time I did, I opened another space to heal.

APRIL

It was heartbreaking to watch Lauren that first year without her brother. Nathan was busy and boisterous and without him, it was ghostly quiet. The two of them were always playing and laughing together, and now Lauren seemed lost. Michael and I had not planned to have anymore children. We were content with Lauren and Nathan, and felt our family was complete, so when I suggested that we have another child, Michael was resistant. He was deeply overwhelmed with grief like me, and to him another child would detract from honoring his only son.

Part of the sadness I felt was that Lauren was now an only child, and I didn't want this for her. It took time to convince Michael, even though I was persistent and impatient. A few months later, after many conversations, we began trying. I am not sure how I focused on falling pregnant while I faced the loss of Nathan. In a way, it distracted me from the intensity of my grief by giving me a focus on new life, instead of facing death each day.

Six months after trying, and nearly one year after Nathan died, we discovered I was pregnant, and bought a new house. Even though we were happy, it was tainted with sadness, knowing Nathan was not there.

As my pregnancy progressed, I realized I was hoping for another boy. I became obsessed that I was having a boy. I could see Michael was hoping for this too, and I began to realize that these thoughts were not good for us. I think, on some level, because we were still deep in our grief, we had created another illusion; that somehow, Nathan would return to us.

Then the ultrasound scan showed us we were having a girl. If we had had a boy, I think we would have conditioned this child to be like Nathan. We would have commented on the similarities, and he would have lived in the shadow of what Nathan could have become. Not everyone who loses a child has an opportunity to have another. For us, it was truly a gift but not a requisite for healing. I met a family who lost their only daughter and son in a car accident. They were not able to have anymore children because of their ages, but they went on to share their heartfelt story in high schools. Their motivation was to help other young teenagers become aware of how easily car accidents can happen. They wanted to make a difference and this way they could honor their children.

The day April was born was an emotional day for all of us. Her arrival lit up our world. When I first watched Lauren hold April, I knew we had made the right decision. Lauren was the perfect big sister, and from the moment they met, they were close. We started to feel hope again that we could walk this journey and begin to heal after the immense loss of Nathan. We believed that April was sent to us as a blessing from Nathan. From a very young age, she dreamt about him and told us stories that she could have never known. From as young as three years old, she would wake up and tell me about a boy in her dreams. She would describe Nathan and his personality, and she would tell me that he made her laugh. She would talk about him as anyone would an old friend, and this always gave us comfort that Nathan was still with us.

HOW MANY CHILDREN?

"There comes a time when one must take a position that is neither safe, nor politic, nor popular, but he must take it because conscience tells him it is right."
Martin Luther King Jr.

About a year after Nathan died, I found myself struggling when people asked me, "How many children do you have?" If I answered three children—which included Nathan—then the next questions would be, "Where do they go to school?" or "How old are they?" leaving me in a difficult position. If I lied, it would lead our conversation into other lies. But if I told them that my son had died, they often asked, "Oh, I'm so sorry. How did he die?" and so began the story of his death and the heaviness of my grief.

So after a series of awkward and uneasy conversations with many people, I made a decision. If I felt that I wanted to share about my son's death, then I would say I had three children. If I was speaking with someone I didn't know, or who I would not see again, I would not mention that I had a son. The telling and retelling of his tragedy was exhausting. Overall, what motivated me to speak of Nathan was not to get sympathy. It was to acknowledge him as real and make some sense of my life. I needed to tell people Nathan *did* exist, that he was my son, and I was proud of him. There is no right way to do this; this was just what I decided. Social situations were difficult to work around at times. It was important to tell myself that I would *always* be his mother and I would always hold the precious memories of my son in my heart, no matter what I said to others. I knew too that with children the topic of many casual conversations, people who did not know me would not really be concerned with how many children I had and it was a relief not to explain my story over and over again.

In my heart, I began to know what felt right for me. Sometimes, there were reasons for sharing my story, and there were times that my story had the power to touch someone's life. Becoming aware of my intuition helped me discern these situations and navigate these conversations with a little more ease over the years. By determining to stay present and connected, I have felt guided to share my story of Nathan at the right time, and in the right place.

PART TWO

SLOWING DOWN

> *"The trouble is you think*
> *you have time."*
> Buddha

I had been living with the loss of Nathan for five years but there were many layers to this grief. I saw that it didn't matter how much I thought I knew myself, when I faced this immense loss, it became vital that I listen to and nurture my physical, emotional and spiritual needs. In the early stages, I felt disconnected from my body. I ignored the signs of fatigue or pain that my body gave me, and felt numb and detached from life. At times, I didn't know what to expect next. Only once I started to piece my feelings together and understand what I needed did I slowly begin to feel reconnected to my body, the people around me, and the world.

During the earlier stages of my grief, I was overwhelmed by my thoughts, and my body received little attention. Often, I was blind to the toll my emotions were taking on me. Only in hindsight could I see that the grief I felt after Nathan died, was the most stressful and all-consuming emotional experience of my life. I discovered during this time that stress causes many forms of sickness. So often people who are diagnosed with cancer or other serious diseases discover their illnesses only after they have slowed down or finally take a holiday.

Nurturing my health over time became a practice of carefully balancing my mind, body, and spirit. I needed to learn that my physical and mental wellbeing were not separate, but deeply interdependent on one another. Of course, not everyone who is stressed or grieving automatically gets sick, but my personal experience was that when I ignored or suppressed strong feelings or emotions, my body expressed this as a physical problem. How often did I feel tired, exhausted, and run down, only to tell myself, *I cannot stop* or *if I don't do it, no one else will?* As I learned to respect my body and nurture myself regularly, I learned that taking a short break is easier than enduring a long haul in bed, or—worse still—in hospital.

Following the court case after Nathan's accident, two things happened in 2005. The driver was not charged, nor was she fined for her part in the accident. Secondly, our attorney told us we had an option to claim for third party accident insurance. In order to receive a payout, we had to prove that Nathan's death had caused us pain, suffering, and a loss of income. While we were able to prove this easily, there was never going to be any compensation for our son's death. We were only eligible for a payout if our health was damaged or if the accident had affected our ability to work in the future. In fact, if Nathan had hurt himself physically and survived, he would have been entitled to compensation. This ruling felt wrong on many levels. Why was their no value attributed to Nathan's life?

After several meetings with our attorney, we were awarded a settlement of $50,000, paid as compensation from our third party insurance. It did not make us happy because no amount of money or compensation was ever going to replace our son's precious life. Once we received the money, we wanted to use it in a way that would honor Nathan. We did not want to buy anything material with it, including paying off our mortgage. We focused on ideas that would create an opportunity for our family to experience something together. Michael and I had always wanted to travel, but we didn't want to go on a short trip as tourists. We wanted to find a place where we could slow down and begin to heal. We were tired of fighting for justice, tired of carrying the heaviness of our grief, and tired of pretending that everything was okay. We settled on the idea of moving to Italy for nine months because it seemed like a welcomed relief.

Michael and I both loved the idea of Italy, because of the importance Italian people place on family. Not long after we had made our decision, we started to make plans for this immense change, and in 2007, we chose a little town in Tuscany called Panzano—a quaint village between Sienna and Florence.

Once we were there, I finally understood how busy our life in Australia was, and how much I had been suppressing my emotions about Nathan's death. It had been stressful packing up and leaving home with so much to organize. Combined with our grief, we were exhausted. It wasn't until we had finalized our plans to live overseas that I finally understood how this constant stress was affecting my health.

A few weeks into our trip, I woke up and found I was having difficulty swallowing. My throat was raw and swollen. It felt like I had tonsillitis but it didn't improve with time. Any dreams of living

La Dolce Vita soon came crumbling down. Here I was surrounded by beautiful food, wine, and produce and I couldn't even swallow. I was reluctant to see a doctor because of the language barrier, and eventually found a doctor who spoke English, although we had some strange conversations, until I was finally diagnosed with acid reflux. My Italian doctor also suspected that I had developed a stomach ulcer, but he said he couldn't be sure.

I tried a few types of medications, which the doctor prescribed. I emailed my Australian doctor for advice too but unfortunately nothing seemed to relieve my symptoms. Having suffered these symptoms for about six weeks, I decided to try some more holistic approaches. I changed my diet and started to think differently. I tried to understand why I was not improving and I spoke to my sister, Lynn, who lives in Perth. Lynn had been learning about energy healing and how our emotions affect our health. She suggested that the reflux could be a side effect of my grief. She sent me a book on healing that helped me understand my body and its energy systems. Lynn also suggested yoga as a way to release some of my deepest emotions.

During the previous year back home in Australia, I had also developed another close friendship with a beautiful energy healer, Sa. She emailed me in Italy with lots of information about acid reflux and explained how I could work with my body, mind, and spirit to heal. The morning after I had spoken to my sister about yoga, I began my daily practice. At first, it wasn't for long. I downloaded poses from the internet, but learning to do yoga on my own instead of in a class was difficult. I also changed my diet and ate mostly organically grown food.

On those days I didn't feel like doing anything, I always pushed past my initial feelings and stayed committed to the practice. I wanted to feel better and I knew it took time to see results. I found that, over time, holistic healing happened when there are subtle shifts in our bodies and energy systems. At first, it felt like nothing was happening, but I remained disciplined and could see that if I was ever to heal, it would take small steps, each and every day.

When I practiced yoga, I used my breath to release an emotion within. Each time, I felt lighter and less constricted in my throat. After several months, and by the time we had left Italy, I was almost cured. I felt a much greater awareness of my body, its strength, and its own determination to heal. Obviously, medical intervention was extremely important when I was very sick but when medicine is combined with holistic therapies such as acupuncture, reiki, chiropractic care, and yoga, there were remarkable physical and emotional transformations.

When I was grieving, it was essential that I learn how to nurture myself. Stress and sadness lowered my immune systems, and so it was vital that I listened to the signs my body gave me, especially when I felt utterly and emotionally drained.

Strategies for Nurturing

- Making time for stillness and solitude.
- Keeping well-hydrated and eating nourishing food.
- Sleeping and resting are essential for recovery, especially during the early stages of grief. When sleeping patterns are disturbed, it's important to have a rest each day.
- Allowing others to offer support with meals and daily help.
- If the body says it's unwell, listen to it. Being proactive is better than being reactive.

- Staying up-to-date and regular with physical and mental health check-ups, and talking openly with doctors or therapists.
- Exercising. Walking and yoga are gentle healing exercises that strengthen the body and give the mind a break from the symptoms of grief.
- Reading and learning about grief to discover more about the different ways to heal.

FACING MY FEARS

There is nothing to fear other than my mind.
Shantideva

I n the first few months after Nathan's death, I felt a new kind of fear arise in me. My nights were restless from insomnia, bad dreams, and intrusive memories of the accident. This sense of fear and the constant lack of decent sleep made me feel weak. An old teaching from the great African savannahs (*Run to the Roar: Coaching to Overcome Fear* by Paul Assaiante and James Zug) tells a story about facing fear. It helped me understand that if I kept running from or ignoring my fears, I would never reach a place where I could heal and feel safe. The story begins with a herd of animals eating their way across the plains of Africa. The lions wait in the tall grass nearby and anticipate the chance to prey upon the grazing animals. The lions prepare for their hunt by sending the oldest and weakest members of the pride away from the rest of the hunters. They were the ones who had lost much of their strength and most of their teeth but their roars were, by far, the most resounding. The old lions settled in the grass, directly across from where the stronger lions waited and watched. The grazing herd entered the area between the hunting pack and the old lions, and the old ones roared mightily. At the sound of the roar, the herd panicked. Blinded by fear, they turned and fled from the source of danger but instead rushed wildly into the place where the strongest lions waited in the tall grass. There, they faced their deaths.

When I was caught up in my fear, I was unable to see clearly. I stopped moving toward my potential. Fear created a sense of panic and caused me to run away and hide. I felt fear manifest in physical symptoms as well. Anxiety gave me symptoms like a faster heartbeat, dizziness, sweating palms, and an overwhelming sense that I would die. Whenever I felt this anxiety, I wanted to run. I wanted to run towards anything except the feelings I was having. I wanted to find a place where I would feel safe; a place that would keep me from facing my pain. It is a natural instinct to run. The fight or flight response is a physiological reaction to a perceived harmful event or attack. Even though I wasn't being attacked or harmed, my body was constantly reacting as if it was.

I could see I needed to face the roar of my fear. I knew that once I summoned the courage, I could run towards it. I started to heal when I tried something different. Instead of reacting to feelings of anxiety by running away, I started to control how I breathed. As soon as I felt my anxiety build, I began to breathe deeply. With each breath, I calmed my thoughts and softened the tension and stress in my muscles. I started to breathe deeply and slowly. The power of my breath helped my anxiety pass. I could not control when my anxiety would strike but I could control how long it stayed.

At first, it felt uncomfortable but with time and persistence, I started to trust the process. I discovered I could sit still with my fear and control how it affected me physically. With practice, I no longer found myself fighting or resisting these feelings. My confidence grew. As I took control of my fears, they no longer had control over me. By dealing with my fears I became aware of the messages I was sending to my mind and my body, and I became aware of the self-talk that was feeding my fears. I allowed myself to experience the sense of loss and despair in every bone in my body. I no longer denied my feelings or ran away from them. Over time, the fear dissipated.

When I questioned my fears, I saw the lies I was telling myself. At its core, I could see I was afraid of the unknown. I questioned, *How will I cope with all these emotions?* or *How will I deal with my grief and guilt?*

When I became disciplined at practicing stillness, I started to calm my busy mind and I could finally see a way through. I started to write in a journal which helped focus my thoughts.

Questions that Guided Me

- *What are my fears?*
- *When did they begin?*
- *Where in my body are these fears manifesting?*
- *What happens to me when fear is expressed?*
- *Are these feelings controlling me?*
- *How can I shift these feelings when anxiety takes over?*

A Meditation for Fear

I am clear in my mind about what I am afraid of. I am aware of my self-talk. I visualize being afraid and anxious, and see myself handling the situation in a calm and clear manner.

I place the palm of my hand on my stomach and one hand over my heart. Begin breathing slowly and deeply.

I notice how my breath calms me and connects me.

I allow my feelings to be present.

I notice how the intensity passes when I allow myself to breathe deeply.

Even if I cannot identify my fears, I allow myself to be still with my feelings, and allow them to pass.

YOGA

"Yoga is not about self-improvement; it's about self-acceptance."
Gurmukh

I went to my first yoga class after a friend suggested I come along, about six months after Nathan's death. My mind and emotional state were constantly being haunted by the 'what ifs' so I decided to give it a try. There are many dimensions to yoga, and it turned out to be a powerful step in my healing. I learned that yoga is an ancient system of philosophies, principles, and practices, derived from Vedic traditions of India and the Himalayas over 2,500 years ago. It relates primarily to the nature and workings of the mind, and is based on practice and self-enquiry.

Yoga cultivates health and well-being—physical, emotional, mental, and social—through regular practice and a range of techniques. These include postures and movement, breath awareness and breathing exercises, relaxation and concentration.

At first, I was reluctant with yoga. My friend wanted to take me to a popular style of class called Bikram, where the class was held in a heated room for 90 minutes, which to me, seemed like a very long time. I was overwhelmed during my first class, but afterwards, I experienced a complete sense of peace and lightness, and that night I dreamt that Nathan was happy and safe. At the end of the dream, he kissed me on the cheek and I woke up with a distinct feeling of hope.

After that, I began going to yoga regularly. Initially, yoga invited me to focus inward, and I'd had trouble doing that previously. Yoga helped me slow down my busy mind, something else I had been struggling to do, but when I connected to my breath in class and I breathed more deeply, I felt more relaxed. Yoga poses that opened my chest allowed me to open up my feelings of grief and helped me let them go. Eventually, I practiced the techniques I was learning outside of class and I felt stronger. After a few months, I still had days where grief overwhelmed me, but yoga eased my emotional heaviness and I found I had more energy.

With time, I began to see that each pose in yoga helped my body release its stress. It also allowed me to be more open to receive love and healing. Yoga helped me understand when to nurture and when to rest my body. When I practiced being still in yoga, I had time to listen to my thoughts, allowing my emotions to surface, instead of suppressing them. I learned to feel my pain and accept it without judgment. My yoga practice helped me start to understand, from a fresh perspective, that I had no control over the day Nathan died. In understanding that from a deeper more bodily manner, I began to face one day at a time. I began to choose not to live in the pain of yesterday or the fear of tomorrow. And that is how I began to cope.

Types of Yoga

Bikram

Bikram yoga is practiced in a room heated to $40^{\circ c}$ ($104^{\circ F}$). Classes run for 90 minutes and consist of the same series of 26 postures, including two breathing exercises. It is a highly-disciplined yoga, but the heat is good for the muscles and has a certain appeal. Bikram was my first yoga class and, after this, the rest seemed easy.

Hatha

Hatha—'ha' meaning 'sun' and 'tha' meaning 'moon'. This refers to the balance of the masculine and feminine aspects within all persons. The masculine relates to the active, hot sun; and the feminine is the receptive, cool moon. Hatha yoga is a path toward creating balance and uniting opposites and toward developing a balance of strength and flexibility in the body. Techniques also teach students to balance the effort and the surrender in each pose.

Hatha yoga is a powerful tool for self-transformation. It asks practitioners to bring attention to the breath, which helps still the fluctuations of the mind and be more present in the unfolding of each moment.

Vinyasa

Vinyasa means 'connection'. In Vinyasa yoga, each movement is synchronized to the breath. Vinyasa is a term that covers a broad range of yoga classes. It is sometimes also called flow yoga, because of the smooth way that the poses run together and become almost like a dance. The breath is all-important and the teacher instructs students to move from one pose to the next as they inhale or exhale.

Kundalini

Kundalini refers to the energy of the 'root chakra', which comprises the area of the lower spine. Classes are generally very intense and focus on the core muscle area.

Kundalini yoga is based on a series of asanas, or poses. Each asana is done with a specific breathing technique that intensifies the effects of the poses. The purpose of each pose is to free energy in the lower body. Kundalini sequences, which are called kriyas, may consist of rapid, repetitive movements performed in conjunction with a designated breathing method or holding a pose while breathing in a particular way.

Ashtanga

Ashtanga is commonly called 'power yoga' or 'classical yoga'. It is physically demanding and best suited to ex-athletes or people looking to really push their bodies.

Ivengar

With Ivengar, there are lots of props, such as blocks, harnesses, straps, and cushions. There is a lot of focus on good alignment, which makes Iyengar ideal for physical therapy. It is also invigorating and energetic.

Restorative

Restorative yoga is gentle on the body. The poses are slow and relaxed and there is a focus on breathing that helps quiet the mind and release stress. I love this style of yoga because it balances emotions and energy. It is gentle and perfect for beginners. Restorative yoga helps release tightness and replenishes the energy that grief takes from us.

Strategies to Start Yoga

- Find a studio and teacher that feels comfortable.
- Explore different types of yoga, find one that suits your body and your fitness level.
- Be patient. It can be difficult at first to be still while in pain and with a busy mind.
- Be nurtured while working through this change in life and slowly cultivate an ability to see a bigger picture for the future.
- Don't give up after one class. Like any new activity or practice, it can take up to three months to really start to see changes. It takes time to really see an overall improved outlook on life.
- Trust that yoga will lessen the fog and busyness of the mind, providing a clearer path to healing.

MEDITATION

> *"Peace comes from within,*
> *do not seek without."*
> Siddhartha Gautama

After practicing yoga for a few years, my next lessons to follow arose from the practice of meditation. Through meditation, my understanding of grief deepened. When I understood meditation, I discovered it did not have to be difficult. It did not need to be practiced for hours each day in the lotus position, but rather it is a practice of mindfulness, one that helped me stop and listen. It allowed me to focus on other parts of my life besides death and the heaviness of grief. The simple acts of becoming aware of my breath and being still to feel my emotions allowed me to understand the meaning of mindfulness, and this gave me a deeper awareness of how I could heal.

Meditation is best explained as spending time in stillness. It was sitting quietly, listening and understanding my needs. The foundation of all forms of meditation is cultivating a calm and positive state of mind. Through regular practice, my mind felt calmer and I learned to focus on what is important. At times, it helped me experience a profound sense of peace. Meditation connected me to the deepest parts of myself—exactly where I held my grief. It also encouraged me to develop concentration and gain better clarity about grief. This helped improve a sense of positivity and eventually helped me to see the truth of my situation more calmly.

Before I started my meditation practice, I was taught to understand that my practice is not a performance and it doesn't need to be evaluated as neither good nor bad. I learned to recognize and let go of my overwhelming thoughts, and part of this is releasing judgment. Meditation also taught me to surrender to the pain of my emotions and to let them go. When I was busy in my mind, I lost connection to my feelings and they became more unpredictable. With meditation, I learned to experience them and released them with focus and discipline.

At first, meditating wasn't easy. I was constantly distracted by thoughts and felt like my attempts were failures. It was uncomfortable at first, but I persevered with a daily practice and, within a few months, I experienced a shift in my stress levels and my sense of grief. At the end of each day, I saw that I was calmer, and my mind wasn't overwhelmed by a tangle of emotions.

The Benefits of Meditation

- It decreased tension-related pain, such as headaches, insomnia, muscle and joint problems.
- Meditation helped me physically. Every time I felt stressed, I understood I was increasing my chance of getting sick. The headaches, digestion problems, and insomnia I experienced

improved significantly when I proactively listened to my body and slowed down when I needed to.

- It increased energy levels as I gained an inner source of energy, improving my immune system and vitality.
- As meditation increased my energy, I was able to give much more emotional support to Lauren and Michael. This became a major catalyst for our family to heal together.

The power of meditation is that it brings brainwave patterns into the restful alpha state that promotes healing. The body calms and rests for a moment and the mind becomes fresh, delicate, and beautiful. Meditation also increases the levels of the hormone melatonin in your body which regulates our body's internal clock and sleep cycles.

Sara Lazar, a neuroscientist at Massachusetts General Hospital and Harvard Medical School, was one of the first scientists to take the anecdotal claims about the benefits of meditation and mindfulness, and test them in brain scans. In her research, data showed evidence that there were changes in the brain after just eight weeks of practicing meditation.

The amygdala, the fight or flight part of the brain which is important for anxiety, fear, and stress in general, got smaller in the group that went through the mindfulness-based stress reduction program. Meditation also allowed significant decreases in stress, depression, anxiety, pain, and insomnia, and contributed to an increased quality of life.

A Practice Meditation

I find a quiet comfortable place to sit in nature—on the grass is best—but any room on the ground floor is fine as well.

Sitting straight and relaxed, I close my eyes and take some deep breaths in and out slowly. I begin to feel relaxed, still and present.

I am aware of the ground beneath me and my body sitting upon it. I feel the solidness of the ground around my lower body; I feel the strength underneath me.

I focus on my body and how it feels. I scan my body to check for heaviness or tightness.

I feel and focus on these areas and breathe into them slowly. I feel the difference as the breath helps me release and soften them.

With any emotional heaviness I am feeling—maybe in the throat or the heart—I consciously feel it and then start to breathe deeply and slowly through my body out into the earth, releasing anything I am holding, releasing any stress or tension with each breath. I visualize my breath releasing these feelings and any tension into the earth.

I keep practicing this until I feel lighter and the heaviness diminishes.

Breathe deeply and relax.

LAYERS OF GRIEF

« Whatever you are not changing,
you are choosing. »
Laurie Buchanan

Through a practice of daily meditation, I began to understand and see myself differently. I became aware of the need to accept who I had become after Nathan's death, and to accept that grief was revealing the many layers within me. My attitude about everything changed: what was important before the accident grew unimportant, what I felt I could not live without before that day became useless and meaningless.

Facing death also created new questions and beliefs about my role in this world. At first I resisted this change and longed for everything to go back the way it was. As my reality set in, I began to search for ways to move gently forward and to understand who I was without Nathan. Throughout the years, I began to understand that it was my acceptance of Nathan's death that helped lightened my grief and help me live fully.

While there were the initial emotions of shock and grief, I found as I deepened my practice, I learned to accept the new life I had been given and that my healing would continue over a lifetime.

There were times, however, when I convinced myself that I had fully healed. I would think, *That doesn't bother me anymore*, only to be triggered again by an innocent comment or a reminder of the past. This too, I learned, was a natural part of the process. I also had to face up to my anger or unhappiness within my relationships. When I blamed people or my circumstances for my negative emotions, I began to see it was just me, still holding on. Once I realized it was me who needed to heal and change, I began to experience it.

Strategies that Helped

- When emotions of grief or stress were triggered, I made time to understand why. When I ignored them, stress and grief just kept arriving in different situations. I allowed myself to take time and connect to my feelings. In stillness, I would try to understand this pattern within me. I asked myself questions like:
  ○ *Have I felt like this before?*
  ○ *Do I want to change this? Do I want a different outcome?*
  ○ *If not, why?*
  ○ *Did I need to allow forgiveness for others or myself?*
  ○ *What belief do I need to release in order to feel lighter?*
  ○ *How would that make me feel? Who am I without this belief?*
  ○ *Will my outcome be different when I change the way I approach my situation?*

These questions are confronting, but when practiced in stillness, I learned how to answer them honestly and I began to understand who I was. I started to see that when I changed my thoughts and beliefs, I changed my outcomes and I was responsible for this change.

FORGIVENESS

"Out beyond ideas of wrong doing and right doing, there is a field. I will meet you there."
Rumi

During my grief, I experienced strong feelings of anger and resentment. At times, it was too painful to let go of these emotions because I was convinced an injustice had been done. I directed these emotions towards the driver of the car that had hit my son. Over time, this increased my anger rather than decreased it. I was consumed by thoughts of justice for my son and I wanted the driver to feel my pain. However, she wasn't remorseful or apologetic for her part in Nathan's death, and this made everything worse. We took the driver to court, convinced we could charge her with speeding; convinced that if we punished her on some level, we would feel better. In the end, she was not charged, and no matter what we did, I never got any relief or sense of justice. In fact, it just left me more frustrated. After about a year, I could see I needed to forgive the driver and release my anger.

I took my time and thought about this very seriously, and decided to write the driver a letter to tell her I had forgiven her. It surprised me how ready I was to do this, because I believed I would always feel anger towards her. When I completed the letter, I felt an immense relief. I immediately felt lighter and it gave me a sense of power knowing I was capable of this. I understood that this act of forgiveness was ultimately for me. It lessened the toxic grip anger had upon me, and this allowed me to focus energy in other areas of my life. When I let go of the anger, I created more space within. As I accepted that forgiveness was not going to change my past, I discovered that it would enhance my future. When I forgave the driver, I forgave myself, and when I sent the driver thoughts of peace, I received peace as well. There is no right time to do this; only I could come to this understanding when I was ready.

At first, I did not want to forgive the driver. I allowed myself time to understand why I felt the way I was and I knew there would be a right time to explore the concept of letting go. In working through forgiveness for the driver, I decided to write a letter. Expressing my feelings in a journal was helpful as well. I understood that I did not have to send my letter, but when I did, I did not send it with conditions or expectations. When I decided to forgive the driver, I was doing it for myself. In my case, the driver did not reply or respond to our family after the accident.

Studies have found forgiveness to be associated with improving health. It helps alleviate the physical symptoms of sleep fatigue and somatic complaints. Forgiveness restores positive thoughts, feelings, and behaviors and this has a healing impact on our overall health. Buddha said, "Holding onto anger is like grasping a hot coal with the intent of throwing it at someone else; you are the one who gets burned." Forgiveness helped me find peace, empowered me, and allowed me to heal another layer of grief.

GUILT

"Guilt is the source of sorrows,
the avenging fiend that follows us
behind with whips and stings."
Nicholas Rowe

Forgiving the driver was the first layer of forgiveness, but as time passed, I became aware that I was carrying a great deal of guilt and I knew it was important to face this and allow forgiveness for myself. After Nathan died, I focused on memories that reminded me of what I had not done for him, like the night before he died when he asked me to be with him, or the times I was frustrated with him when he tested my patience. These thoughts left me feeling heavy. I felt I needed to punish myself for the choices I had made; and by holding onto these burdens, my mind lived in the past. Releasing these thoughts through forgiveness did not seem possible at first. On some level, I believed if I let them go, I might lose my memories and connection with Nathan. When I thought about forgiving myself for these past experiences, I felt there would be nothing left to hold onto. Forgiving myself meant moving into the future without Nathan and this scared me.

Strategies to Let Go of Guilt

- *Writing*—not long after Nathan died, I started to journal. It really helped me express my feelings and understand why I felt the way I did. I started by writing down my overwhelming thoughts and feelings and allowing myself to express everything without judgment. I took time to read it back. I asked myself some questions:
  - *Do I need to hold onto to these thoughts and feelings anymore?*
  - *How would changing these thoughts or feelings make a difference in my life?*
  - *How is guilt holding me back?*

- I answered honestly and began to see where I could change the thoughts and beliefs I had about my situation. Then I started writing down some new goals. I wrote out affirmations and new thoughts I could have each day and made time to practice them. Keeping a journal helped me release, learn and track my progress and goals for the future.
- *Visualization and Forgiveness*—sitting in a calm, quiet place, I visualize the person I feel guilty about and ask for forgiveness. I see him or her forgiving me, as I see both of us covered in light and no longer burdened by guilt.

Through these exercises, I could see that my guilt often had more to do with me than the situation I imagined. It was often a self-created reminder of all the things we wish we had done differently.

I came to see that I was the only one who could change these feelings of guilt and when I gave myself permission to stop feeling guilty, I was able to lighten my heaviness and be much more present with my family and my friends.

For Us
by Karen Lang

For us to learn, we must let go of our need to be right.
For us to disconnect from busyness, we must learn to
become still.
For us to find our truth, we must surrender our control.
For us to heal, we must admit we are sick.
For us to live fully, we must accept that we will die.

JUDGMENT

*CLove is the only force capable
of transforming an enemy into a
friend.*

Martin Luther King Jr.

Often, when I felt stuck in life, I began to judge myself and created self-doubt. Before I understood that the way we grieve is individual, I found that anytime I compared myself to others or worried about their judgments of me, I lost vital energy.

When I adopted assumptions about where I should be along my journey or when I should accept Nathan's death, it did not help me. Grieving at my own pace was important in the first few years.

Strategies that Helped Suspend Judgment

- Validating my feelings; knowing it was okay to feel bad about my situation and not know what to do next.
- Identifying and refraining from judging or having negative thoughts or feelings about myself.

- Spending time alone in nature, so that I could listen and find my own answers.
- Allow myself time to enjoy life, even during grief.
- Finding a motivation and a discipline that can help me get up and take one step at a time.
- Listening to and respecting my inner-self and intuition.
- Reassuring myself that the intensity of grief would lessen overtime.
- Reminding myself of all the wonderful things that have happened in my life and when Nathan was with me.
- Being grateful for the little (and big) things in my life.

The more I compared myself to others, the more I told myself I was not good enough. When I didn't feel good enough, I felt isolated.

When I learned to have compassion for myself, judgment simply lost its strength. Although judgment is a natural instinct, when I became aware of my thoughts that carried me away into negative thinking, I learned to change it. Each day was as beautiful as I allowed it to be.

ACCEPTANCE

«Life is a series of natural and spontaneous changes. Don't resist them; that only creates sorrow. Let reality be reality. Let things flow naturally forward in whatever way they like. »

Lao Tzu

How do we begin to accept the death of our child? At first, this seemed impossible and it took years to adjust to the pain and emptiness after losing Nathan. Looking towards the future, to a new life without him, was overwhelming; living in the past meant I had to conjure illusions while living in the present was unknown and empty.

Finding some kind of control in a situation that was entirely outside of my control took time to process. For a time, it meant adapting to the pain and disconnection each day and it meant slowly accepting that Nathan would never be with us again, one day at a time.

Dr Elisabeth Kübler-Ross MD, pioneered methods in the support of personal trauma, grief and grieving, associated with death and dying. She also dramatically improved the understanding and practices in relation to bereavement and hospice care. Her ideas, notably the five stages of grief model (denial, anger, bargaining, depression, acceptance) published in *On Death and Dying,* do not necessarily arrive in this order, however, it is a guideline to help navigate the many layers and of grief.

- *First Stage: Denial*—in this stage, I was reluctant to accept that Nathan was never coming home. It felt as though I was experiencing a bad dream, that the loss was unreal, and I was waiting to 'wake up' as if from a dream, expecting that things would be normal.
- *Second Stage: Anger*—it was shortly after I began to accept his death that I began to feel anger at the loss and the unfairness of it. I wanted the driver to be punished and a flood of emotions surfaced during this time. I wanted someone else to take the enormity of my grief away.
- *Third Stage: Bargaining*—in this stage, I started to hope that he would return and that maybe if we had decided not to take Nathan off his life support we could have found a way. This phase usually involves promises of better behavior or significant life change which will be made in exchange for the reversal of the loss.
- *Fourth Stage: Depression*—once it became clear that anger and bargaining were not going to reverse the loss, I felt the weight of my reality and had to confront the inevitability of my loss and my own helplessness to change it. During this period, I cried more, experienced sleeping changes and withdrew from others while I processed this truth.
- *Firth Stage: Acceptance*—finally over many years and working through my emotions, I began to enter a stage of acceptance. I was still processing my grief and emotions, and I realized that this would be over my life time, but in this stage I was

able to accept that the loss has occurred and could not be undone. I began to plan for my future without Nathan and re-engage daily life.

Strategies that Helped Develop Acceptance

- *Acknowledge the Emotions*—this meant if I needed to cry or scream, I did. If I needed to retreat, I did. If I felt like laughing or wanted to be happy, I could.
- *Nurture the Sense of Fragility and Feelings of Helplessness*—when I felt fragile or helpless, I couldn't be with a lot of people. I had to say no to social events and the pressure from friends "to stay strong". I nurtured these overwhelming feelings with rest and quiet days.
- *Be Patient and Allow Time to Adjust*—some days were easier than others. Some days I felt frustrated with the complexity of my feelings. I wanted to change this journey and return to the life I knew. It took many months for me to adjust.
- *Following The Gift of My Instincts and Doing What Is Right for Me*—there was a lot of advice given to me on the days that I felt vulnerable. Doing what was right for me became essential in my healing. I had to let go of any pressure and be true to myself.
- *Take One Day at a Time and Accept Each Moment with Compassion*—I placed a lot of pressure on myself to be strong. This did not serve me. When I accepted I felt weak and was in immense pain, it allowed me to progress. It helped me find compassion for myself and to accept my pain.

The more I avoided how I felt in the present moment, which was fraught with pain or difficulty, the more I separated myself from experiencing any kind of acceptance. Consciously and sometimes with great effort, I had to allow myself to feel what I was feeling in certain moments. When I accepted my feelings, I knew it was all I could do under the circumstances. And it was enough.

From acceptance, I began to relax and allow my emotions to surface rather than resist these feelings and suppress them. This is a monumental task when we have lost a precious child, but when we learn to practice acceptance, we grow into ourselves and our journey.

A Meditation to Release Heavy Emotions

Sit quietly in nature or in a quiet room.

I become aware of my breathing and take slow even breaths until I feel myself relax.

I imagine I am sitting on the beach before the sea.

I visualize the sun overhead and the ocean and the waves coming in and out, close to me.

I connect to my feelings and all that I am holding emotionally. I feel my heart's pain and loss.

I wait there. I take some deep breaths in and out again. I know that these feelings will not overpower me. I know these feelings are part of me. I allow them to be present.

I see that the tide is turning. I see that each wave grows a little more distant as it slides along the beach, then returns to the sea.

I see the tide retreating into the ocean and feel it take my heavy feelings.

I feel them being released into the vastness of the ocean.

I use each exhalation to let go.

I use each inhalation to stay present.

I imagine as the tide retreats into the ocean, that my heavy feelings are leaving me too. The sun shines overhead, filling this new space within me with light.

I feel these emotions being released into the vastness of the ocean.

RIPPLE EFFECT

"Just as ripples spread out when a single pebble is dropped into the water, the actions of individuals can have far-reaching effects."
Dalai Lama

During my grief, I was often unaware of all the emotions I was carrying. Sometimes, it was anger or sadness; other times, resentment or guilt. It wasn't until I started to release the burden of these emotions that I understood how heavy they were.

We are all connected; what affected me, affected those around me. When Nathan died, his death rippled throughout the community. We never imagined the affect it had on so many.

One particular lady had seen his photo in the local paper. After she had read the article and kept the paper for a while, she had a dilemma. She didn't feel it was right to throw his picture out. Instead, she cut it out of the paper, placed it in a photo frame and posted it to me. She said that this photo belonged to me. I cried when I received it.

The taekwondo and rugby union clubs both created awards in honor of Nathan. These achievement awards are handed out to other young boys each year. This gesture meant so much to us.

I received a thank you card from one of the organ recipients. She wrote about the courageous decision we made to donate Nathan's organs and told us that the kidney she had received enabled her to experience a full life with her children and husband. Her gratitude was immense and I was grateful she shared it with me.

Other people were burdened by Nathan's death as it triggered their own unresolved pain. Some people experienced great pain, reminders of their own losses and grief, while others were immensely grateful for a new realization of how precious life was.

Growing along my journey through grief I have learned about the importance of connecting with others, and to the energy around me to help heal my wounds. At first, I felt isolated and alone in my grief, I could not believe that anyone could possibly understand how I was feeling. Through the practice of stillness, I learned to feel the energy around me in nature and in those around me. I learned to feel a deep connection to life, to my ancestors who have gone before and for those who would come after me, my children's children. I could see we all play a part in this connection and that we need each other to survive.

With the strength I received from practicing this I became stronger in my understanding of my connectedness to everyone and everything, I was no longer alone.

A Meditation to Feel Connected

Find a quiet place in nature.

With eyes open, I focus my energy on a tree in nature.

My breath slows down my incoming thoughts as I stay focused on the tree.

I notice how many different branches there are on the tree, but they are all connected to the one source—the trunk. These branches cannot survive without the trunk. If they were not connected they would lose their strength and fall.

I focus on the importance of this trunk, how its roots run deep into the earth, within me. I feel my energy connecting to this source.

I start to see the connectedness of every part of this tree: each part needs the other to survive, each part needs the other to help it grow.

I now visualize my connection to everything and everyone in my life. I see the part I play in this connection. I see how important my role in life is and how it effects the whole. I see how when I grow, others grow. I see how when I let go, others let go. I see when I am in pain, others feel this also. Feel the connection to everything.

Breathe it all in.

OUR HOPES

« Although angels do not fly down to open the grave and restore the lost, the days and months come as angels with healing in their wings. »
George S. Merriam

Nathan was only nine when he died and so he wasn't planning a serious career. He did think that he might like to be a demolition man or an actor like Jim Carrey but we were left wondering who he might have become.

Letting go of all the hopes and dreams we had for Nathan was yet another layer we needed to let go of and heal over time.

At the start of my grief, it was difficult to see Nathan's friends. I missed seeing him with them and the fun they used to have. As the years passed, and the boys grew up and moved on with their lives, I realized Nathan would never share in their milestones or have their memories. This took time to accept. I was never jealous of the boys, just sad that Nathan would not share in these experiences.

Still, I allowed myself to have these feelings, and I also learned to let them pass with time. It took patience. I am always interested in what the boys are doing and enjoy hearing about their successes and their lives.

Their health and happiness is exactly what Nathan would have wanted too.

Deep Understanding

by Karen Lang

Do not weep for me
For I feel peace and freedom
I feel immense love which expands far beyond
I now understand everything

Do not weep for me
Rather, be still and breathe through your pain
See how my death has opened your mind
To see all the love, courage, and strength within you

PART THREE

SURVIVAL INSTINCT

"Between stimulus and response, there is a space. In that space is our power to choose our response. In our response lies our growth and our freedom."
Viktor E. Frankl

As humans we are stronger and more capable of surviving than we think. There were times after we had lost Nathan that people said, "I could never cope in your situation," or "This is my greatest fear, I don't know how you do it." Unfortunately, we do not get to choose how our lives unfold, but we do get to choose how we respond to it.

Internationally renowned psychiatrist, Viktor E. Frankl wrote about his experience as an Auschwitz concentration camp inmate during World War II in the 1946 publication of his book, *Man's Search for Meaning*. He also described his psychotherapeutic method, logotherapy, which helped people identify a positive purpose in life and then immersively imagine and engage that outcome.

According to Frankl, the way prisoners imagined the future had a tremendous effect on their longevity. He believed that everything can be taken from a person except one thing: the last of the human freedoms—to choose my attitude in any given circumstances, to choose my own way.

I saw the world differently after Nathan died in 2001. After feeling devastated by his death, I knew I wanted to live differently. I wasn't living badly before however, but I did not question my choices in life. I never wondered if there was more.

And then, everything had changed. Time was more precious than before, and I wanted to understand how I could use my time with more purpose. I craved new meaning, as Frankl cites as one of the greatest drives human beings have, especially after a crisis.

The human instinct is to survive, and I knew I could too. Things could only break me if I allowed them. I understood I had a choice in how I felt. There were times I felt desperate after losing my son but after about five years, I made the choice to change that.

Change was not something I did overnight. It was a daily decision to get up, and help heal my emotional wounds with positive energy and acceptance. I learned that the enormity of my grief was not necessarily the hardest part of my healing. It was embracing all the *little* things that I needed to do in order to step out and change.

Change was difficult, and life didn't always go according to plan. My family's life was completely turned upside down. At first we were overwhelmed with doubt and we couldn't see past our grief. As time passed, I chose a different direction; one that forced me out of everything familiar.

Before Nathan's death, I thought I was in control of my life. When he died, this certainty was taken from me and all I saw were hardships and challenges ahead. While I had no choice in losing Nathan, grief required me to face many decisions. How I approached those decisions determined what road I took.

I chose to slow down my mind. I took on the disciplines of yoga and meditation. I created a different experience of life itself. It wasn't easy. There were times when people said to me, "You could stay in your room and never come out, and no one would question that after losing a child."

But I had to question it.

When I found the courage to shift my focus in another direction, the door opened. Through practice, the path widened and revealed immense opportunities for me. I began to let go of my anger and guilt and this shifted my direction and redefined my dreams. I stepped out and found a deeper understanding of my grief, and my life. This new choice meant I could live authentically.

GRATITUDE

*" Reflect upon your present
blessings, of which every man has
many, not on your past misfortunes,
of which all men have some. "*
Charles Dickens

rief confronts us with many overwhelming emotions,
and in the beginning it is very difficult to find anything
to be grateful for. Because my mind was constantly
filled with thoughts of the past, or were lodged in the future by
fear, I had no room for gratefulness.

Trying to live in the present seemed impossible. It wasn't
until I had been practicing yoga and stillness for some time that
I was able to see the gift in each moment.

At first, grief sent me into a tailspin of emotions and fear, as
I tried to come to grips with Nathan's death. It was hard for me
to see anything good in my life, but my daughter Lauren needed
me to be present and to guide her. She needed to know that
there was hope amidst our pain, and staying present with her
helped me connect to each moment. Children have a wonderful
ability to stay present and it was in the small, precious moments
that I shared with her, where I could find my gratitude.

Feeling my emotions as they surfaced each day was important, and it helped me move through the many stages of grief. Finding hope, even for a moment, gave me strength and courage. It allowed bits of happiness to shine through.

Over time, I could see my situation in a different light. Of course not every day was like this. It took time and patience. Some days, I sat in darkness not ever imagining there could be healing or light beyond my pain. It takes strength to look for the light; it takes courage to step out and rediscover gratitude.

In my search to heal, I discovered that there is an endless supply of love, peace and hope but we cannot give this to one another. We have to find and feel this in ourselves.

A Meditation for Gratitude

I find a quiet spot and become conscious of my breathing.

Allowing my mind to let go and be still, I feel myself become present in this moment, accepting it exactly as it is.

I become aware of my feelings and the emotions behind them.

I start to breathe out any heavy feelings that rise up. I accept them all.

A Journal Exercise for Gratitude

- When I feel lighter and more balanced, I can begin to write down what I am thankful for.
- I find one thing each day that I am thankful for and increase it over time.

- It could be 'I am grateful for peace today', or 'I am grateful for my family and their support', or 'I am grateful for my health', or 'I am grateful for my courage today'.
- Every time I say 'I am grateful', I change the energy in my body and my mind and this helps shift my heavy feelings.

Grateful

by Karen Lang

I am grateful for moments, because they can be taken from you at any time

I am grateful for stillness, because busyness made me forget what was important

I am grateful for love because it has always healed my wounds

I am grateful for knowledge because now I understand how precious life is

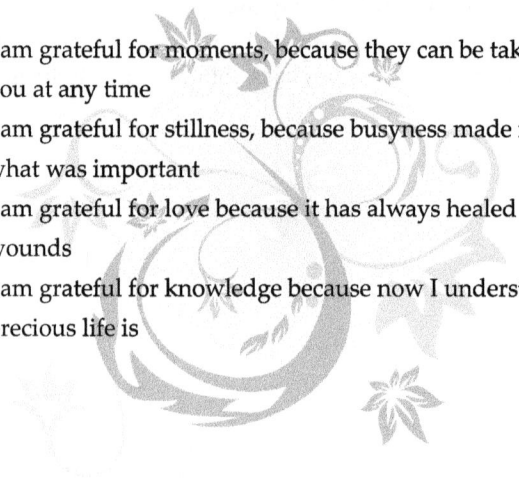

AFFIRMATIONS AND INTENTIONS

"There is no affirmation without the one who affirms. In this sense, everything to which you grant your love is yours."

Ayn Rand

Deliberate clear intentions have the power to change the world. Becoming conscious of setting my intentions each day, rather than relying on habit and the usual way I did things, brought a conscious shift in my attitude and my life. Affirmations strengthened me by helping me believe in the potential of an action I desired to manifest. Much like exercise, they raised the level of feel-good hormones and pushed my brain to form new beliefs and positive thoughts. I noticed that when I verbally affirmed my dreams and ambitions each day, I was instantly empowered with a deep sense of reassurance that my wishful words would become reality.

Combined with stillness, I found practicing affirmations gave me an ability to shift some of the deep sad feelings I had about Nathan's death. It helped shift my focus onto gratefulness and peace, rather than on sadness and despair all the time. Over time, this practice helped me find strength.

Some days will more difficult than others, but when I started to bring in positive energy, I shifted my thought patterns. As I created a discipline of practice each day, bit by bit, I learned to see outside my story and connect to the expansiveness of life. I began to see that no words were empty words, as every syllable I spoke engaged energy towards or against me. If I constantly thought, *I can't*, the energy of these words affirmed a belief. If I thought, *I can!* the universe created the abilities to do just that.

Although it was important that I feel and accept my feelings of grief, I found it also important to give myself permission to feel happiness and joy again as well. Using slow breathing techniques before I started, my affirmations helped me feel calm and centered. Affirmations also work best in the present tense, as they are below. I said them consciously and spoke them confidently, out loud for a deeper effect. 'I am' means we are already there, instead of 'I will be'.

Affirmations

I am love.
I have peace within me.
I have the ability to create new thoughts and beliefs.
I accept this moment and all that it holds.
I accept my loss, sadness, and pain.
I have strength and courage to move forward.
I am present in my grief.
I accept my life as it is now.
I am connected to everything and everyone. I am supported.
I deserve healing, hope, and peace
Today I let go of my old ways and take up new positive thoughts.
I am blessed with abundance and love.

I am grateful for my family and the support I receive.
My potential to succeed is infinite.
I am aware of my self-worth and make choices accordingly.
Affirmations that resonate work best, and allow hope and
positivity to return to my life.

Intentions

Sending out intentions into the world is a powerful act. Over time, I can create new thoughts and beliefs about what I want, and how I can begin attracting that into my life. Owning my life and becoming responsible to live deliberately and with clarity brings our dreams into reality.

I found that creating intentions that were meaningful in my life were the most powerful. Intentions are complete and direct both choices and energy. Positive intentions feel expansive, light, uplifting, joyful, and peaceful. Believing, feeling, and experiencing the manifestation of my intention allow them to be more tangible. Feeling or visualizing the experience I want each day is a good place to start.

Examples of Intention

- Today I will nurture my needs (visualize this happening).
- Today I am grateful for my abundance and the ability to share this.
- Today I feel peace and stillness within me.
- Today I am connected to all that is positive and good.
- Today I am supported and loved.

Try different words and sentences that resonate with you the most. Write them down or use them as a mantra each day.

BREATHING

*"Breathing in, I am calm,
body and mind. Breathing
out, I smile. Dwelling in the
present moment. I know this is
the only moment."*
Thich Nhat Hanh

When I was deep in grief my shoulders were heavy, and I was not breathing deeply. I was unaware how this breathing created more stress in my body. I noticed that when I was stressed, my shoulders went up, my throat constricted, and I breathed shallow breaths. Over time, this felt like a normal state and my body adjusted to it. However, physically, it meant I limited precious oxygen to my organs and over time, when starved of this oxygen, I eventually become unbalanced and unwell.

Becoming conscious of my breathing every day and of the intent to inhale and exhale, helped me let go of what I no longer needed and brought new energy into my body. On a mental and emotional level, holding my breath 'locked in' the feeling I was trying to avoid.

Slow breathing and stillness offers clarity and connection to living in this moment. I saw that a slow, deep breath during any stressful moment instantly changed my perspective and the way I felt. Deep breathing restored my mind and body, allowing my emotions to rise up and be felt. Becoming conscious of my breath and how it locked my body up during grief and stress was one of the first steps in understanding how I could change my feelings.

Breath work practitioners teach us there are six primary emotions sourced in particular areas of the body: joy and sadness in the chest; fear and excitement in the stomach; and anger and passion in the abdomen. Problems in these areas can be contributed to suppressed energy of that emotion.

Breathing Meditation

I sit or lie quietly on the ground.

I become aware of the rise and fall of my chest.

I take a deep breath in and a deep breath out three times.

I notice how I relax with each exhalation.

I become aware of how my body feels.

I feel where there is stress or tightness in my body.

I allow my breath to release this stress or heavy emotions.

I allow my breathing to bring new energy throughout my body.

I feel myself connect to everything.

I feel myself relax into this moment.

CREATIVITY

*« Others have seen what is and
asked why. I have seen what
could be and asked why not. »*
Pablo Picasso

I n 2007, when we were living in Italy, I discovered a deeper
love of writing. I have always enjoyed reading and this
helped me learn so much about healing my grief. While I
had started a journal for Nathan, and wrote ones for Lauren and
April, in Italy I explored writing for myself. It took courage and
took me into a new energy and a lighter vibration.

When I discovered the creative side of writing, I found that I
was able to use words as a way of expressing my grief; something
new to me. It took me a few years before I could see that writing
was the perfect way to express my story and I found that as I
wrote about Nathan's life and death, the words flowed freely.
Writing helped me understand that I had come a long way in
my healing and growing through my grief.

Over time, I decided to take a few courses in writing and
this gave me a desire to learn more and I continue to grow more
confident in my writing. I also started a blog, which gave me a

sense of purpose and vitality amidst my grief. There were times early on in my grief when I felt no inspiration or purpose.

At times I felt stuck and unmotivated. Changing my perception of the situation and creating new ideas and thoughts helped me heal. Creativity ignited passion within me and it helped me express my grief. When I created new ideas, I felt motivated. Writing gave me a new energy and a different focus on grief. I started to see that when I expressed my grief, it not only helped me, but helped others who were unsure of how to begin their journey.

Strategies for Creativity

- *Write a List*—I made a list of everything I loved, including all the things, people, and concepts I was attracted to, passionate about, and interested in without any limits. This list motivated me and helped open my mind.
- *Do the Opposite*—if I felt like I wasn't moving through a heavy time in my grief, I tried to do the opposite of whatever I was doing. If I felt like staying in bed, I would make an effort to move and go for a gentle walk in nature. If I didn't feel like cooking a healthy dinner, I would ask for support and make an effort to eat well. Sometimes doing the opposite, even though we do not feel like it, can help shift our mood.
- *Gain More Energy through Movement*—being uninspired and feeling detached had a physical component and effect on me, which could lead me to being sedentary or feeling slow. To take me out of this physical and mental state, I tried to do activities like yoga and meditation. This often replenished my energy and nurtured my grief. Anything that moves and stretches my body helped clear my mind and gave me more energy.

CREATING SPACE

« If you don't see your heart, if you don't see the divine in you, if you don't see your strength, if you don't see the blessing that this breath is, that is because you are so far away, so far away that you can't see it. Come closer. Come closer to yourself. And you, too, will see what I am talking about. »

Maharaji

Often when I felt disconnected, I lost sight of the immense strength within me. It took me a long time to notice I was doing this. In stillness, I had an opportunity to listen to my needs and to feel my emotions. When I distanced myself from my pain and emotions, it was because I was scared to open the flood gates of loss. For a while, this worked. But it had a cost. When I chose to disconnect from my pain and from my wounds, I also disconnected from receiving love, light, and healing. We cannot have both. When I shut down one area of my body, mind or spirit, the counter affect was that I also shut out receiving. Constricting or shutting down limited my view of a bigger picture. It kept me feeling trapped without hope.

When I learned how to create space within me, I opened myself to receive inspiration, guidance, and direction. I created opportunities to see more and trust there is a way through.

How Do I Constrict?

- Trying to control a timeframe or outcome of my situation
- Allowing fear in which blocks my view
- Being stubborn—believing that my way is the only way
- Refusal to forgive
- Not accepting my situation

How Do I Create Space?

- Meditation, yoga, breathing techniques
- Forgiveness
- Spending time in nature/reconnecting
- Surrendering and accepting my situation
- Letting go of my negativity
- Visualization on positive thoughts and energy

I learned that spending time alone nurturing myself was not shutting down or constricting. It was the perfect space to listen to what I needed. It was only when I shut out my feelings and emotions that I disconnected from receiving too. When I felt sadness, I could also feel joy. When I felt anger, I could also feel peace. If I suppressed anger or sadness, I suppressed the fullness of other emotions too.

When I began living from a place of authenticity, I validated my decisions in life. In doing so, I started to open up and create space for healing. In order for me to create space, I needed to be present with the emotions I had at the time. I became aware that when I did not stop and see the goodness in my life as it was, then I could not find it anywhere else.

It was challenging to accept my present feelings in grief and loss. However, when I lived in acceptance of what was, I learned to appreciate the small gifts I had. I learned to understand that peace and truth were already within me wherever I was. I knew I could travel the world to see and hear prophets and teachers or go to every course offered, but in my busyness to search outside of myself to find the answers, I would miss discovering the treasure within.

LIVING MY TRUTH

"The unexamined life is not worth living."
Socrates

When I lived my truth and spoke from my heart, it opened my path to find wisdom. As I learned to express my feelings of grief, I found I had more energy and understanding towards myself and those around me. Living my truth connected me to my higher-self, which guided me to communicate more deeply.

When I doubted myself, believing that someone else probably knew what to do instead of me, I lost confidence. A lack of confidence did not help me grow or learn. I started to search—how could I trust that I had wisdom and knowledge to know the answers? Stepping out and making my own decisions, whether they were right or wrong, was how I learned. When I worked through my doubts and experienced how far and how wide I could go, I could see my potential. Sometimes the decisions I made seemed wrong or uncomfortable for someone else, but this was how I found what was right for me.

Staying on the same course that I had always known or walking a different course was my choice. It didn't mean I did not consider others in my decisions. I did. Sometimes it took time for others to understand my choices. Sometimes I was supported in them. When I felt lost or unsure about my direction, I sought advice from a mentor or family member. This helped me immensely to get a different point of view and to be guided out of my confusion. When I allowed myself to receive help, it allowed me to see a way through. The more I opened myself to change, the more I lived my truth; it just took practice.

Strategies that Helped

- I allowed my feelings to be shared deeply when I was hurt or angry.
- I created activities to express who I was, through writing, art, drawing, dancing, singing, and giving freely.
- I learned to say "no" when I needed to, and say "yes" when I wanted to.
- I spent time with mentors who affirmed my true nature.
- I stood up for what I believed in and learned to be honest with myself.
- I made mistakes and learned from my experiences.

REFLECTIONS

❝ *Everyone who comes into our life blesses us with the opportunity to forgive, love and accept the parts of ourselves they are mirroring.* **❞**
Sa Silvano

I think one of the most difficult parts of my journey has been confronting the beliefs I held about myself and others. I had often distanced myself from circumstances that challenged me or people who created stress in my life, finding it easier to ignore them. One of the gifts of my journey has been to understand why I encounter these circumstances or people in the first place.

I found that sometimes, I hid different aspects of myself. I did it unconsciously, and so it wasn't easy to acknowledge and confront this truth within me. When I denied this truth, I found I attracted the same types of people, those with the same hidden aspects. They came into my life to show me what I needed to accept, leading me to a deeper understanding of myself. It took courage to face this. When I began to notice an irritating behavior in someone else, I took the time to understand that this may be within me also. Once I found myself struggling with a competitive friend. This friend was someone who was always trying to outdo me or be better than me. I asked myself, *Is there a competitive spirit within me? Do I express this towards others?* It didn't take long before I could see my own competitive nature more clearly.

Other character traits such as anger, feeling superior, sadness, laziness or selfishness were all traits to be explored. Whatever I disliked in another was also a part of me. Once I acknowledged and accepted this truth, I could start to change it. Naturally, this applies to positive attributes as well. When I was kind and compassionate to myself, I mirrored this back to others. When I was honest and nonjudgmental, I also found this in others.

Whatever I was creating in life reflected my belief system. Once I understood this, I brought light and love to this part of myself and began to heal. I was amazed at how quickly my outer world responded to this change. I found that the person that was challenging me either moved away from my situation, or didn't seem to bother me anymore. Some parts are definitely harder to shift than others but I was patient in nurturing and accepting this process. I saw that these wounds may have been carried for a long time, so it was important to give them time to heal.

Strategies to Help Shift these Wounds

- Sitting quietly on the grass or ground at home, I take some deep breaths. I feel where in my body I am feeling tight and blocked. I focus on this area, and send my breath to it.

- I take some deep breaths, and feel myself let go and relax.
- If I can't feel it, then I just keep breathing deeply and allow the anger and hurt to be released with each breath, into the earth or ground.
- Slowly, I see the person I am irritated by or angry with in my mind and forgive them. Breathe deeply. If I need to, I can do this a couple of times. Now I see this person surrounded in light. I breathe deeply.
- I ask myself where is there a need to let go and heal inside of me. I feel where it is and acknowledge it. I forgive myself and breathe deeply.
- Now I see this person with me, surrounded in love and light. I hold that image and breathe deeply.

There is no instant fix for pain and yet, practicing this meditation when needed, helped me release any anger and hurt towards others. It helped me move into a higher understanding of my connection to everyone and the gifts they bring to teach me.

BEING PRESENT

*"Tomorrow is tomorrow.
Future cares have future cures,
and we must mind today."*
Sophocles

The three understandings in being present:

- Knowing only this moment
- Observing
- Compassion

I Only Know This Moment

By understanding that I did not know the future and could not live in the past, I acknowledged there were no fixed certainties in life. This was difficult because I wanted to control my overwhelming feelings of grief and change what had happened. Unfortunately this was not possible.

When I allowed myself to deal with one day at time and not spend time worrying about the future or the past, I felt lighter. Every day was a different day in my grief. Having an attitude of hope each morning that I only had to face one moment at a time gave me a better view of the world and my journey.

Observing Life

Stepping back from the drama and stress in life through stillness is to become an observer. It meant learning to accept who I was in my grief, without feeling the need to judge or change my situation. *Observing* life shifted my perspective.

In the first stages of grief, I found this is difficult to do. Some days I became lost in my guilt and anger, some days I found peace. The practice of observing my feelings and thoughts could only be learned from being in stillness or nature. This helped me become present to all my feelings.

Compassion

Once I practiced the first two, I was naturally drawn to express compassion for myself and then, as a consequence, toward others. As I learned to be kind to myself and nurture my needs, I was able to make choices that were right for me. The compassion I learned to have for myself was instrumental in my healing. It helped me listen and learn to be present in every situation.

Two Practices That Can Help Us Connect

Firstly—A Practice for Breathing

- The breath and the mind flow together. When the breath gets shallow or stressed, so does the mind. When attention is given to the breath and I breathe slowly, the mind is naturally calmed and soothed.
- I sit quietly.

- I allow my breathing to settle. I feel and listen to my breath inhale and exhale.
- With each exhalation, I feel my muscles and my mind relax and allow my thoughts to come in and go.
- I breathe slowly and evenly. I am present with every feeling.

Secondly—A Practice for the Body

- The body reflects physical, emotional, and mental states. Peace and happiness lighten my energy and soften my face but when I feel down, my shoulders and chest collapse and I feel heavy.
- I become aware of my physical body, I check how I am standing or sitting.
- Am I sitting upright and are my shoulders back? Do I have a clear airway for my breath?
- How am I feeling? What are the physical sensations of my body as I connect?
- Now try to change those feelings with positive thoughts and breathing. I breathe deeply and slowly and feel the difference.

As the Chinese philosopher Lao Tzu said, "The journey of a thousand miles begins with one step"; one step of desire to keep moving forward into healing.

PART FOUR

HEALING IN NATURE

*"The best remedy for those who
are afraid, lonely or unhappy is to go
outside. Amidst the simple beauty
of nature, I know that there will
always be comfort for every sorrow,
whatever the circumstances may be.
And I firmly believe that nature
brings solace in all troubles."*

Anne Frank

When I began learning about the healing energy of nature, I understood how important it was to spend time there, replenishing and balancing my energy. I saw that I took the time to charge my phone and fill the car with fuel, and yet, I would forget to replenish my own energy until I was running on empty. When I felt depleted or overwhelmed, I still kept telling myself that I could not find a few minutes a day to allow myself to recharge. Grief took so much energy from me, so it was vital to spend some time in nature to reconnect, and get my strength back.

While I was looking for ways to manage my grief, I found a growing body of science proving that nature is good for us. Spending time in nature, or even looking out the window at a scenic landscape, has great benefits. It has been proven that people who spend time outside four or more times a week are significantly less likely to suffer depression.

Being in nature took the focus away from my pain. Outside, I could breathe more freely. It helped me understand that there was more in life than my grief. Nature also inspired feelings in me, which connected me to others and my environment. Flowers and plants have long been a symbolic part of rituals around death, and so it made sense to spend time in these places of beauty and peace.

On one level, nature provided a frame of reference for death and dying for me. It reminded me that death was a natural process that I could not escape or ignore. Nature gave me solace during my grief and allowed me to process my overwhelming feelings.

Walking with a friend, or alone, helped me clear my mind and let me see the world from a different perspective. Nature's healing properties provided a powerful inspiration to keep going, especially when it felt like the world had ended.

I think that one of the reasons that I felt so disconnected from the earth was that I literally was. I always had my shoes on, separating me from the ground. I found it important to make an effort to take my shoes off and ground myself. By connecting my feet against the cool grass or feeling the sand between my toes at the beach, I connected and received the Earth's beautiful energy.

Just as nature needs sunlight to survive and replenish; so did I. Taking myself outside to get some sunshine and exercise was essential for my mind, body and spirit.

A Meditation in Nature

Sitting quietly in nature amongst the trees, flowers or on a mountain, I take some deep breaths, feeling each exhalation, releasing any heavy energy.

Keeping my eyes open, I become aware of the stillness around me.

I become aware of the sounds and movements in nature.

I notice how nature is always changing, each season bringing death and new growth.

I see myself moving with the different seasons in my life.

I see myself become still, through these changes.

I take a deep breath in and out, relaxing my shoulders.

I feel the stillness and peace within me. Connect.

Listening In Nature

In Australia, our Indigenous people have a special respect for nature. The identity Aboriginal people have with the land and the environment is sacred and unique, and they have a very strong sense of community. Every person matters.

Aboriginal writer Miriam-Rose Ungumerr-Baumann describes how Aboriginal culture teaches people to be still and to wait. They don't try to hurry things up. They let life follow its natural course, much like the seasons. She says the people watch the moon in each of its phases. They wait for the rain to fill their rivers and this helps water the earth. When twilight comes, they prepare for the night. At dawn, they rise with the sun. Aboriginal people watch the bush foods, and wait for them to ripen before they gather them. They wait for the young people to grow, stage by stage, through their initiation ceremonies. And when a family member passes, they spend a long time with their sorrow. They acknowledge their grief, and allow themselves to heal slowly. I felt I had so much to learn from her people and their culture; from their understanding of life and human connection to the environment. Each time I slowed down to connect; each time I listened, I understood that life would provide my every need.

Miriam teaches us the word Dadirri, which when said, recognizes the deep spring that is inside all of us. She says it is a deep calling. We can call on it, and it calls to us. This is the gift I was thirsting for. When I experienced silent awareness or Dadirri I could be made whole again. There is no need for words, Dadirri is listening. To understand Dadirri, I focused on something specific, such as a bird, the grass, a flower, a tree, or clouds in the sky or a body of water, whatever I could see. I could also let something find me, be it an animal, the sound of a bird, the feel of the breeze, the light on a tree trunk. There was no need to try, I just waited and learned to be patient.

Following this quiet time, there was, on occasion, value in expressing in some way my experience of this quiet, still listening. Talking about the experience or keeping a journal, writing poetry, or singing were ways I honored this experience. This needs to be held in balance; however, the key to 'Dadirri' is in simply being, rather than in activity.

Dadirri
by Miriam Rose

To know me
Is to breathe with me
To breathe with me
Is to listen deeply
To listen deeply
Is to connect to everything

SURRENDERING

Some people believe holding on and hanging in there are signs of great strength. However, there are times when it takes much more strength to know when to let go and then do it.
Ann Landers

I am a very impatient person when it comes to achieving my goals or dreams. So often, I have tried to control or speed up the process, rather than allow my life to unfold exactly as it should. It took years to trust and know that life moves on, with or without my help. The energy it took for me to force things depleted me, and pretending I had control did not move me any closer to my dreams.

Each time I learned to surrender to 'what is', however, and accepted my current situation, I understood I was exactly where I needed to be. Sometimes, when I have pursued my goals blindly from a place of ego or selfishness, I was met with resistance. This resistance taught me to step back and assess my situation.

For me, patience required discipline. There were times when I believed that being patient felt like I was not taking action or trying hard enough. I learned, however, that this was not true. Patience has been one of the most crucial disciplines in achieving my goals.

While life shouldn't be about wishing, waiting or resisting, it has been about being present and allowing my life to flow naturally. When I stopped chasing the wrong things, I gave the right things a chance to find me.

I have understood that when an unexpected stress comes into my life, or if I feel I cannot move through an issue, I always have a choice in where my mind travels. If it is into the past, I can have thoughts of judgment, relive a familiar pattern, or think I know the outcome. If it is in the future, I can have thoughts of fear, 'what if' scenarios, or I might feel overwhelmed with what might happen. I gradually came to understand where my mind and thoughts went when I was under stress. When I became present, I found that I did not have any fear. I did not worry about what has been because I accepted I did not know what was next, and that anything could move if I allowed it.

By understanding and practicing this mind shift, I created a different space. I found I had more clarity, and I knew what to do.

Strategies to Achieve Your Goals

- When I wish to achieve a goal or dream in life, it's important I have clear intentions.
- I write down or visualize what it is I want in life.
- I write down the steps I need to take to make this happen.
- I write down the actions I need to do each day.
- Once I understand clearly what needs to be done, I start the process the next day.

- I keep visualizing what I would like, but I do not attach any time wondering when or how this will happen—I will not know.
- I let go and allow.
- When I feel unmotivated, I read back on my initial steps.
- Every day is a new day to start again.
- Every day is a chance for my life to change.
- I am patient and consistent in my visualization, and I surrender—it takes time to create dreams.

Surrender

by Karen Lang

Surrender to what is
Move with the ebb and flow of life
Allow yourself to be where you are
Resistance creates barriers
Surrender to what is

EXPECTATIONS

"Expectation is the root of all heartache."
William Shakespeare

From the moment I began to trust in my inner-mind power, I became aware of the power I had to solve my problems. It was the moment when I became aware that I could create different thought patterns, even amidst my pain and grief.

During my grief and loss, there were times when I was drawn into a pattern of negative thinking. Sometimes, I felt like grief was holding me captive and had made me a prisoner of my own mind. There is nothing negative about simply reflecting on past experiences. This is how I learned and grew through my grief. But negativity arises when I dwelled on a situation repeatedly with no real intention to let it go. At those times, I felt trapped.

Early in my grief, my mind was not open or aware of thoughts coming in and out but over time, I began to try to understand it. I thought about how the mind has two parts: the conscious mind, and the unconscious mind. The conscious mind is everything that is inside awareness, including feelings, emotions, sensations, memories, perceptions, or anything that can be thought about or discussed. The unconscious mind is everything that is outside of awareness. I began to see that I could only change my unconscious impulses once I became aware of my conscious thoughts.

Types of Negative Thinking

- *All or Nothing*—"I have to do things perfectly, because anything less than perfect is a failure."
- *Disqualifying Any Positives*—"Life feels like one disappointment after another."
- *Negative Self-Labelling*—"I feel like a failure. I'm flawed. If people knew the real me, they wouldn't like me."

I saw that negative thinking was an obstacle to self-change. When I could see that my thoughts were affecting how I perceived my life, I began to see how I could change them. I became aware that what I expected in life had the ability to create a positive or a negative outcome. So if I expected my life to be filled with grief and heartache, then that's what it was. However if I expected that I had the power to create change and positive thinking, then that would happen.

I changed my old patterns of needing approval and discovered that I had my own unique power and wisdom. I only began to understand this when I became conscious and aware of my thoughts and how I spoke to myself. Knowing that I could not blame my circumstances or those around me was the first step in taking responsibility. It allowed me to recognize the amazing power of my mind and how I could transform my dreams into reality.

Strategies to Let Go of Negativity

- *Stillness*—without stillness, I can't listen to or become aware of my expectations, thoughts and desires.
- *Practice*—becoming aware of how often I spoke negatively to myself or about my grief was something I developed through practice over many years. Each time I changed my thought patterns, I felt more clarity and peace.
- *Affirmations, Intentions and Mantras*—these strategies helped rewire my mind and let go of old patterns and conditioned thoughts but it took patience and daily persistence.
- *Visualization*—when I practiced stillness, I was able to learn how to visualize the life I wanted. I learned that I didn't have to know when or how that would happen. I just needed to create it in my mind and expect it.
- *Never Give Up*—being impatient for change prevented me from moving through each layer of grief. Each day I had a new opportunity to discipline myself and start again.

Each time I saw my practice turn into positive results, my confidence and trust grew. After many years, I saw that changing my perception of every situation gave me immense power. Each time I expected more, I created more. Each time I believed *I have the ability to do this*, I received what I needed.

STAY OPEN

"Our mind has a door. A password can open it. That word is stored safely in our heart, waiting for our willingness to retrieve it."
Unknown

The greatest lesson in my life has been to live with an open heart and mind, because this always led me to awareness and learning. I suffered when I developed a strong attachment to my views or the wrong perceptions.

When I simply opened my heart, I was surprised by my inner strength. When I became flexible and open to others' insights and experiences, my mind began to expand. This meant connecting or listening to people that I admired. Once I let go of how I thought my life should evolve, I saw everything from a different perspective.

The heart is expansive, intuitive and creative. When my heart is opened, my mind is quiet. When I allowed myself to be deeply moved or touched, I experienced an expansion of love and understanding. I began to see that my true power grew when I released resistance. When I let go of my beliefs about grief and life, I opened my heart to receive peace and comfort. Each time I allowed myself to let go, my energy expanded.

Over time, and with practice, I began to view the world and others with more compassion and understanding. These feelings gave me more energy and opened me to new possibilities. When I expanded my level of awareness, I tapped into my inner power and became aware I could create a new vibrant reality of wellbeing and health.

The only way to achieve this understanding was through discipline and practice. Every day, I created time to listen and to be open to receive. Awareness, I found, wasn't passive. Action was required to connect to my inner truth.

Strategies to Stay Open

- *Be Passionate*—I found things I was passionate about and loved doing. Each time I choose to live deeply and creatively, I opened the door to my heart and my truth.
- *Remain Open*—when I searched for teachers that could open my mind and heart, I began to expand my knowledge and awareness. I connected to like-minded people and created space within my heart to receive the right support and love.
- *Take Responsibility*—finding time to practice each day required discipline. I realized that this could only happen when I chose to do things differently. Once I took full responsibility for this, I connected to my power and strength.
- *Redefine Yourself Everyday*—every day was a new day for me to step forward. Some days were harder than others. Instead of negatively judging myself those days, I practiced letting them go, and I gave myself permission to start again.

The heart is the center of feeling and love and it represents the true self. I learned that a fulfilled life has love, joy and gratitude. Kindness and compassion began within each person. When I nurtured the desire to love and accept myself in life, I opened my heart to make wise choices, and this helped fulfill my needs.

SELF-LOVE

«Life is not happening to
you; it's responding to you.»
Unknown

One of the most difficult challenges I had to endure after Nathan's death was learning to embrace my own self-love. When I connected to my divine nature, I could learn to love everything within me, and all things became possible. I had always struggled with self-love. Even as a little girl, I lacked self-confidence. I was shy and often doubted my ability to achieve anything. My self-talk and beliefs often limited me from stepping out into the unknown and discovering my potential.

Inspirational speaker and author Abraham Hicks said that anytime we compare ourselves to others—on any level—we erode our self-love. When I wished that I was someone else or I wanted my situation to change, I was not connecting to love or my natural energetic vibration. Learning to love the everyday experiences in life and the people around me became the key to unlocking this feeling of love's vibration. Each time I embraced who I was in the moment and accepted my situation, I deepened my connection to my inner spirit.

I learned that when I had expectations of receiving this love from anything or anyone, it resulted in a never-ending quest. This made me feel trapped and unable to connect to the power I had to create change. The moment I understood I could change my perception of every situation was the moment I connected to my power.

At first, coming to terms with Nathan's death seemed impossible. It did not seem natural for my child to die before me, but the truth is, he did. When I consciously acted with compassion and kindness about my situation, I began to feel momentum and flow. When I resisted my situation, I blocked this flow and allowed fear in. The greatest lesson in life is to learn to love, and to be loved in return.

Developing Self-Love

- Remember to be gentle with yourself and take one day at a time.
- Become conscious of your thoughts and understand your fears.
- Practice accepting and loving each moment as it is.
- Attend courses or listen to talks that help remind you to find this love within.
- Understand that *you are love*. You do not need to search for this in other people or things.
- Feel love and appreciation in everything you think, do, and say.
- Love the food you eat. Love the work you do. Love every moment you are alive.
- Each time we consciously do this, we connect to the vibration of love.

TRANSFORMATION

*" Life isn't waiting for the
storm to pass...Its learning to
dance in the rain. "*
Unknown

I always thought that life needed to be perfect for me to be happy. I believed that if I acted perfectly and had perfect children, I would be in control of my life and be able to predict its outcomes. Nathan's death showed me that this perception was not grounded in truth or reality.

Just as butterflies earn their wings through great effort, so too was my process of change after losing Nathan. It was extremely painful, and it was never without loss or sacrifice. If I was to transform from my old life into another, then a part of me needed to die. Letting go is never easy. Life required me to keep looking within and until I understood and accepted this, I felt trapped in my resistance to change. Sometimes I needed to let go of low self-worth, a relationship, a dream, or an illusion. No matter what it was, transformation could not take place without it.

Motivational speaker Les Brown wrote, "There will be times in our life when we stand at a precipice of a decision." He gives us an example of this choice: A man, who is at the crossroads of his life, is given two choices. He can either go through a door that says 'unknown', or stand in front of a firing squad. The man hesitates and asks, "What is behind the door?"

The leader replies, "You won't know until you walk through it." Feeling overwhelmed by fear and the uncertainty of the unknown, the man chooses to go in front of the firing squad simply because he knows what the outcome will be. The next day, an onlooker walks over and asks the leader, "What is behind the door?"

The leader replied, "Freedom."

Transformation takes courage. Doing what I had always done and believing I knew what was ahead, did not allow me to grow. When I stepped through the unknown door of life, I learned to let go of what I had always known, and it was there that I found my answers and peace.

I may not have felt strong enough to step out in faith and yet, if I waited for that perfect moment to arrive, I may have missed great opportunities that changed the course of my life.

Walking along my journey of grief, I was challenged many times. Each time I had the courage to walk through another door, I discovered my inner strength and was able to take another step towards freedom.

I named my book *Courage* because of the strength it took to walk this long journey of grief. Finding courage each morning helped me to connect to my power and to learn to identify and ask for what I needed. Courage taught me to face and express my pain. The energy of courage reminded me to stand in my truth and do what was right for me. Sometimes I did not understand why my life changed so drastically, but even though I found myself in the middle of the nowhere, it was exactly the right place for me to find my true purpose and understanding of life.

COMMITMENT

“ Once a man has made a commitment to a way of life, he puts the greatest strength in the world behind him. It's something we call heart power. Once a man has made this commitment, nothing will stop him short of success. ”
Vincent Lombardi

A chieving even the simplest of goals required me to learn the meaning of commitment. Time and time again, it was always my commitment that was tested while I was grieving.

From the moment I lost Nathan, I had a choice: to walk towards healing, or to fall into a hole of sadness and pain.

When I thought about it, everything I had ever achieved sprouted from a commitment I made; whether it was having children, completing a diploma, a job, marriage, or even paying off and maintaining a house. Learning how to commit to something is not simply about making the commitment, it's about keeping those commitments, especially in the face of unforeseen pain and adversity.

In my commitment to work through grief, I never saw the finishing line. Often I had to walk blindly into the unknown and, at times, this frightened me. Every day, I made a decision to do my best with what I was given. I began to understand that as I moved through the many phases of grief, it began to lighten. Moving through gently and slowly allowed me to move out of my heaviness.

I learned to train my mind, body and spirit to adapt. I knew that if I pursued a select sport then I needed to train my body. If I pursued a new career, I needed to train my mind. And if I pursued my spirituality, I needed to change my beliefs. It is the same with my grief. I was committed to search for ways to understand my grief. I wanted to learn how to cope with my ever-changing emotions. I was committed to finding stories of hope.

Strategies for Commitment

- *Dedication*—I dedicated time to find the information I needed. I listened to talks about grief. I talked to people who had grieved before. I read many books on grief:
  - ○ *When the Bough Breaks by Judith R. Bernstein* (1998)
  - ○ *On Children and Death* by Elisabeth Kubler-Ross (1983)
  - ○ *Beyond Tears: Living after Losing a Child* by Ellen Mitchell, with Carol Barkin (2005)
  - ○ *When Mourning comes* by William B. Silverman, a prominent Rabbi, and Kenneth M. Cinnamon, a clinical psychologist (2006)
- *Stay Focused*—I practiced disciplines that helped me stay focused on my commitment, like yoga, meditation, and walking in nature.
- *Be Compassionate*—I gave myself permission to fall and fail. Some days I felt hopeless and lost, and other days I felt motivated and committed. I learned not to judge myself.

- *Support*—I created a network of support. I called upon mentors and family to support me and encourage me, when I felt weak and uncertain. I let go of my ego and learned to listen to those who could guide me back onto the right path.
- *View Progress*—grief was a rollercoaster. I did not always know what would happen next, and so it was important to remember where I had been. Recording my progress in a journal helped me reflect on my progress and motivated me to keep going.

Let there be no illusions about commitment. It takes effort and a conscious choice each day.

HAPPINESS

Riches, prestige, everything can be lost. But the happiness in your heart can only be dimmed; it will always be there as long as you live, to make you happy again. As long as you can look fearlessly at the sky, you'll know that you're pure within, and will find happiness once more.

Anne Frank

After Nathan died, it was difficult for me to believe I could ever be happy again. It did become possible, however, thanks to the gifts of time and learning to let go of my emotional burdens.

Throughout my journey, I punished myself with heavy emotions like guilt and sadness. At times, I convinced myself that I didn't deserve happiness or joy. I had to learn to give myself permission again.

Nathan was always happy and energetic. He thought life was exciting, and every morning he would jump out of bed and plan how to make the most of each day. These positive qualities helped remind me to find that energy again and to live more fully.

I understood to create happiness, I needed to take chances, appreciate the special memories I had with Nathan, and learn from my past mistakes. Nathan's death made me realize how precious and short life can be. Knowing this, I began to question why I was denying myself happiness and joy.

In losing someone I loved, my grief took over and it became very difficult to find time to enjoy life. I realized I had to feel and heal my grief first. I understood if I denied my sadness, I also denied my happiness. To help me heal emotionally, it was important that I made an effort to do activities that boosted my spirit and energy. If I wanted to find happiness I needed to eliminate any darkness or negativity in myself.

In the beginning, I found exercise helped shift my stress. Walking, yoga, and aerobics all helped me release heavy energy and increased my stamina.

Research tells us that the trauma of loss can stimulate creativity which in turn leads to new opportunities for happiness and success. Writing helped me express my pain and my story, and this has opened another door to my happiness.

I learned that being happy did not mean that everything was perfect. When I learned to accept my emotions and look beyond my pain, I saw a bigger picture. I realized I could affect change by transforming the only thing that I had control over, and that was myself. By practicing this, I felt hope.

It took effort. I didn't want to pretend I was happy; I wanted to allow happiness back in. I made sure to find activities that connected me to happiness. Sometimes it was just being spontaneous, like dancing with my children, or watching a funny movie. Sometimes it was being creative and open. Sometimes it was just accepting who I was while I was grieving.

Making every moment count and appreciating what I had helped me heal. In the end, I knew I wouldn't be remembered for how long I mourned my child. I would be remembered for what I loved and the passion I had for my life. I want to continue to pursue and find this love within me. When I am in touch with this special space, I always find it feeds out to those around me. This is happiness.

Life presents its purpose and beauty in unexpected ways. My experience has taught me that I am stronger than I think, and there is always a way through every situation.

Our life's successes are measured by the opportunities we have to share our joy with those we love, and the way we honor the lives of those who have left us.

CHAKRAS AND ENERGY HEALING

" The whole universe appears as a dynamic web of inseparable energy patterns. Thus we are not separated parts of a whole. We are a whole. "
Barbara Ann

I n 2008, I started studying Reiki and energy healing. I had been living with my grief for seven years. After my experiences in Italy, I wanted to gain a deeper knowledge and understanding of my body and its emotions. I loved learning about the energy systems within us and around us, and was fascinated by the power I had to change them.

I began to learn that chakras were energy centers within the body where energy flows. There are seven main chakras and they act like a filtration system which allows energy to flow easily throughout the body. If energy flow is unrestricted, the body's health is usually good. Chakra is a Sanskrit word that means circle or wheel. They are spinning vibrating circles of energy that appear as wheels, connecting the physical, mental, emotional, and spiritual dimensions within the body. Each energetic center aligns with a certain part of the body and each has its own symbol, color, and unique vibration. Being conscious of the chakras developed my awareness of the state of my health.

Written knowledge of the chakra system is based on yoga philosophy, which goes back thousands of years. It is written about in ancient texts, such as the Vedas and the Yoga Sutras. Knowing that this energy system was within my body was vital for healing myself and others. It helped me understand my thoughts and feelings more deeply. By practicing Reiki—a type of energy healing—I learned to recognize the feeling and sensation of a blocked or flowing chakra.

I began to understand while working through my grief I could learn to know that when the body's energy system becomes blocked, it usually presents itself on a physical level through a health condition or disease. As I became more aware of the physical, mental, and spiritual parts of my body, the more I became aware of my needs. The mental body includes the feelings and emotions. And in the spiritual body, dwells the intuition and awareness of life. Healing the mind is the same as healing our energy.

When I became aware of, and present to, my feelings and emotions, I developed a connection to my inner thoughts and intuition. Intuition allowed me to understand what to do next, or to know on a deeper level why my life was not working for me. Once I felt this awareness in my mind, body, and spirit, my view on life expanded.

Once my thinking and perceptions about life began to change, it was amazing how other things started to change too. I realized the so-called domino effect always began with me. When I became determined that I wanted to feel better— that I wanted to heal—I began creating positive energy within and around me. I decided to be open to teachers, books, and fulfilling my own potential. Each of us has a purpose to fulfill, and it is up to each of us to find what that is. I became aware of the power of my thoughts and feelings.

Inspiration motivated me. New energies found expression within me, and my desire to move in this new direction, finally outweighed the heaviness of my grief as I began to see my life in a new way.

If you have a deeper interest in the energy systems within our body and mind, I highly recommend the following books:

- *The Book of Chakras* by Ambika Walters
- *Chakra Awakening* by Margaret Ann Lembo

CONCLUSION

The death of a child changes our lives forever. From my own experiences with death I have learned that if we are to heal, we cannot ignore our deep feelings of grief. Instead, we must journey through it all, sometimes on the side roads and sometimes plowing directly into its raw center. For all who face the death of a child…

I wish you enough sun to keep your attitude bright

I wish you enough rain to appreciate the sun more

I wish you enough happiness to keep your spirit alive

I wish you enough pain so that the smallest joys in life appear much bigger

I wish you enough gain to satisfy your wanting

I wish you enough loss to appreciate all that you possess

I wish you enough hello's to get you through the final goodbye

GRIEF SUPPORT RESOURCES

Australian Centre for Grief and Bereavement
Free Call: 1800 642066

Lifeline Australia
24hr Telephone Crisis Support: 13 11 14

Counseling GriefLine Nationally in Australia
Phone: 1300 845 745

Grief and Loss Counseling, Brisbane
To book an appointment with a psychologist or counselor
Phone: 3088 5422 (Mt Gravatt)
3067 9129 (Loganholme)

Seasons For Growth
Offers programs for children, young adults, and adults who have experienced
significant change or loss.
New South Wales, Australia.
Phone: (02) 89122700
England, Wales, Scotland, Ireland.
Contact: info@seasonforgrowth.co.uk
Auckland. Contact: deliar@cda.org.nz

The Compassionate Friends, Queensland
Phone: (07) 3254 2657
Contact: email-support@compassionatefriendsqld.org.au.

The Compassionate Friends, United States
1000 Jorie Blvd. Suite 140, Oak Brook, IL 60523
Phone: (630) 990-0010 or toll-free (877) 969-0010
Contact: terry@compassionatefriends.org

ACKNOWLEDGMENTS

I would like to honor and thank those that helped shape and complete my book:

Firstly to my beautiful family, Michael, Lauren, and April—thank you for your love, patience, and support during the journey of my book. It means everything to me, and you bring so much joy to my life each day.

To Mum, Dad, and my two wonderful sisters, Sheryl and Lynn, who never stopped encouraging me—thank you for your love and support.

I would like to thank Michael's parents and family for their encouragement and support.

To my wonderful network of friends far and wide, who are always there with me on this journey—thank you, you are all important to me.

To my friend, Kate Egerton—thank you for your creative editing and ability to help my story evolve, and for your belief in its potential.

To Lauren Daniels—thank you for your positive encouragement and vision for my book. Your patience and skill with structuring and editing my book has completed it beautifully.

To Miriam Rose—thank you for giving me permission to include your beautiful work in my book.

To the Elisabeth Kübler-Ross Foundation—thank you for your permission to include her work and wisdom in my book.

To Ocean Reeve and the wonderful team at InHouse Publishing—thank you for creating the final touches on my book and for bringing it to life.

Finally, to each and every person that played an important part along the journey of my book—my heartfelt thanks for your time, love, and support.

REFERENCES

Dr. Elisabeth Kübler-Ross
  On Children and Death (1997)
  On Death and Dying (1969)

By arrangement with The Elisabeth Kübler-Ross Family LP and The Barbara Hogenson Agency. All rights reserved. For more information about Dr. Elisabeth Kübler-Ross, please visit: http://www.ekrfoundation.org

Les Brown. https://www.youtube.com/watch?v=GrhsVU6-3rc

Miriam Rose Ungunmerr-Baumann. Aboriginal writer. 'Dadirri' poem, http://www.creativespirits.info/aboriginalculture/education/deep-listening-dadirri
  Miriam is an artist, a writer, and a tribal elder. She works in a non-profit organization working to empower Indigenous youth through education, art, culture, and opportunity.
  Contact: enquiries@miriamrosefoundation.org.au.

Paul Assaiante and James Zug. *Run to the Roar - Coaching to Overcome Fear*. November 24, 2010

Viktor E Frankl: *Man's Search for Meaning* (1946)

FURTHER READING

Courageous Dreaming by Alberto Villoldo, PH.D (2008) Hay House

Pearls from the Heart by Sa Silvano (2013) Ganesha Imprints

The Alchemist by Paul Coelho (1993) Harper Collins

The Power On Now by Eckhart Tolle (2000) Hachette Australia

The Tibetan Book Of Living and Dying by Soygal Rinpoche (2002) Random House

Women Who Run With Wolves by Clarissa Pinkola Estes, PhD (1995) Random House

Yoga For You by Tara Fraser

You Can Heal Your Life by Louise Hay (1999) Hay House

ABOUT THE AUTHOR

Embracing core values of understanding and empathy, Karen's passion as a counselor lies in what she sees as 'the story behind the story'. She strives to unfold each one of her clients' stories and help them discover their true purpose and potential.

She writes a blog, *Healing your Grief*, which addresses an array of wellbeing topics including grief and forgiveness. She also practices yoga and extends her own spiritual practice by teaching weekly meditation classes. Karen lives in Queensland, Australia. She has a Diploma in Counseling.

Find Karen's blog *Healing your Grief* at
https://shamanismandhealing.wordpress.com

For more information about Karen's publications and book tours go to www.karenlangauthor.com

www.ingramcontent.com/pod-product-compliance
Lightning Source LLC
Chambersburg PA
CBHW072122020426
42334CB00018B/1686